D1452011

THE
GRETSCH
BOOK

TONY BACON & PAUL DAY

The Gretsch Book
A complete history of Gretsch electric guitars
by Tony Bacon & Paul Day

GPI Books
An imprint of Miller Freeman Books, San Francisco

Published in the UK by Balafon Books, an imprint of Outline Press Ltd,
115J Cleveland Street, London W1P 5PN, England.

First American Edition 1996
Published in the United States by Miller Freeman Books,
600 Harrison Street, San Francisco, CA 94107
Publishers of GPI Books and *Bass Player* magazine
A member of the United Newspapers Group

ISBN 0-87930-408-1

Printed in China

Art Director: Nigel Osborne
Design: Sally Stockwell
Photography: Miki Slingsby
Editor: Siobhan Pascoe
Typesetting by Type Technique, London W1
Print and origination by Regent Publishing Services

96 97 98 99 00 5 4 3 2 1

CONTENTS

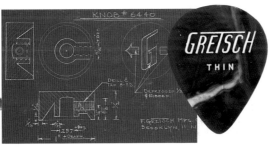
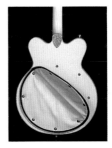

INTRODUCTION

It was in the 1950s and 1960s that Gretsch shook up the world of electric guitars by pouring out colorful instruments loaded with wild gadgets and great names. The Gretsch Book examines the entire span of this company's exceptional history, bringing you the full story of everything from the Country Gentleman to the White Falcon, from G-brands to Filter'Trons, and from big jazz boxes to rockabilly rebels.

Gretsch first came to the attention of the wider guitar-playing public when the New York company formed an inspired allegiance with country picking ace Chet Atkins, whose 'signature' guitars transformed Gretsch's fortunes and firmly established them among the leading ranks of electric guitar manufacturers. In the 1960s George Harrison – a Chet Atkins fan – used Gretsch guitars in the studio and on stage with the world's most famous pop group, and Gretsch hit peak production levels to fill a new demand. Takeovers, slumps and revivals later, Gretsch is once again busy in the 1990s, and our story runs full circle.

You'll also find in this book an unrivaled photographic gallery of rare and unusual Gretsch guitars, all specially photographed for this book and including instruments owned by Chet Atkins, Duane Eddy and George Harrison. Toward the back is a comprehensive reference section designed to overcome the confusion that many players and collectors experience when trying to identify guitars from this 'difficult' brand, complete with detailed listings of every Gretsch electric guitar issued from 1939 to the present.

Most of all, we hope that you'll take pleasure in joining us as we try to capture in words and pictures the spirit of what the company described without fail and with justified pride as 'That Great Gretsch Sound'.

TONY BACON & PAUL DAY, ENGLAND, JANUARY 1996

"When the shadows grow/And the lights are low/Then I play on my Gretsch guitar/
As I touch the strings/Like a voice it sings/It's the voice of my love afar."
Dick Sanford & Clarke Van Ness FROM THEIR 1940 SONG 'WHEN I PLAY
ON MY GRETSCH GUITAR'

"I was *so* thrilled to have my name on a guitar, like Les Paul had his
name on the Gibson."
Chet Atkins COMPLETES HIS 'SIGNATURE' GRETSCH DEAL IN THE MID 1950s...
AND PULLS LEVEL WITH AN OLD RIVAL

"First time I picked up the red Gretsch it just took to me, settled right in
there. There's times it does get twangy, other times it gets smooth and
dragging and menacing."
Duane Eddy DESCRIBES THE VARIETY OF MOODS HE'S ACHIEVED SINCE 1957
WITH HIS FAMOUS GRETSCH HOLLOW BODY MODEL

"I have a feeling the White Falcon was his dream guitar, and I remember when he
was developing it there was talk that this was going to be something real special."
Jennifer Cohen RECALLS HER FATHER JIMMIE WEBSTER'S WORK ON THE FABULOUS AND
DECIDEDLY SPECIAL GRETSCH WHITE FALCON

"We should have had shares..."
George Harrison ANALYSES THE BEATLES' EFFECT ON GRETSCH'S BUSINESS
IN THE 1960s

"Gretsch is my country guitar."
Steve Stills WHO WITH CROSBY STILLS & NASH (& YOUNG) DID MUCH TO REPOPULARIZE
GRETSCH IN THE 1970s

"The guitars look just like the coveted Gretsch models from the 1950s but with
technical improvements designed for the playing style of the 1990s."
Fred Gretsch III EXPLAINS THE 'OLD PLUS NEW' PHILOSOPHY OF
TODAY'S GRETSCH OPERATION

THIS PAGE: *A beautiful Gretsch Chet Atkins Hollow Body from 1960 (left); two headstocks (below) from a 1954 Electro II (left) and a 1955 White Falcon. The Gretsch building (above) in Brooklyn, New York, served the company as factory and HQ from 1916 until closure in the early 1970s.*
OPPOSITE PAGE: *Chet Atkins (left), the most important endorser of Gretsch guitars, with a top-selling Country Gentleman; Gretsch founder Friedrich Gretsch (top left) is next to his son Fred Gretsch Sr., while Gretsch demonstrator/inventor Jimmie Webster serenades company boss Fred Gretsch Jr. in 1951 (center), with Jimmie's business cards close by. Ray Butts (far right) invented Gretsch's famous Filter'Tron humbucker pickups; Phil Grant (bottom left) and Duke Kramer (right) ran Gretsch's New York and Chicago offices from the 1940s to the 1970s.*

guitar division

jimmie webster

fred gretsch mfg. co.
brooklyn. n. y.

REPRESENTING GRETSCH GUITARS

JIMMIE WEBSTER
GUITAR STYLIST
"TOUCH SYSTEM"

THE FRED. GRETSCH MFG. CO.
60 BROADWAY
BROOKLYN 11, N. Y.

IN THE MIDDLE DECADES of the 19th century the proportion of foreign-born immigrants in the United States rose dramatically, with Germany well ahead of Italy, Ireland, Russia and Scandinavia as the main source of this massive injection of new blood. One such middle-class German émigré was Friedrich Gretsch, the son of a grocer from Mannheim, a city that lies between Frankfurt and Stuttgart in central Germany.

Friedrich was only 16 when in 1872 he arrived in the US. After settling in New York City he took a job with a drum and banjo manufacturer, Albert Houdlett & Son, despite the fact that his Uncle William, with whom he lived in Brooklyn, had a successful wine business in the city. Clearly Friedrich was determined to go his own way. He further staked his independence by anglicizing his first name, and in 1883 left Houdlett to set up his own business, the Fred Gretsch Manufacturing Company. He produced drums, banjos, tambourines and toy instruments at the firm's small premises on Middleton Street, Brooklyn, selling to local musical instrument wholesalers such as Bruno or Wurlitzer.

Friedrich's son Fred, the eldest of seven children, had been born in 1880, and at age 15 had a surprisingly swift and unanticipated introduction to his father's music business. Friedrich had returned to Germany with a brother in April 1895 for the first time since his emigration, but while in Heidelberg he died suddenly, aged just 39. Another son, Louis, later recalled the shock of his father's unexpected demise: "The first word the family received after he sailed for Europe was a cable reporting his death and burial."

Friedrich's widow, Rosa Gretsch, is said to have been largely responsible for deciding that 15 year-old Fred should leave his studies at Wright's Business College for an immediate and practical immersion into the real world of commerce. Teenager Fred found himself heading up a still modest operation with about a dozen employees, now based in a converted wooden stable on South 4th Street. There is a story that whenever Fred Gretsch took a customer to lunch in a nearby Brooklyn bar, the waiter would take one look at the youngster and say, "No matter what you order, you're going to drink milk."

Fred seems to have largely ignored what today might be considered ageist remarks, and made a virtue of his youth by channeling teenage enthusiasm into the growth and expansion of the Fred Gretsch Manufacturing Company. Apparently he would regularly venture out onto the roof of the building to help with the tanning of hides for drum skins. By 1900 Fred – usually referred to as Fred Sr. – had added mandolins to the company's drum and banjo making activities. Gretsch's original cable address DRUMJOLIN attests to this early trio of manufacturing interests, and Fred had also begun to organize the importing of musical instruments from Europe, for example introducing K Zildjian cymbals to the American market. Also at this time he moved the company to better premises in a small three-story building once again on Middleton Street in Brooklyn.

On Broadway

Two of Fred Sr.'s brothers joined him in the business after the turn of the century: Louis Gretsch went on the road selling instruments for a year before giving up his one-third interest to go into real estate, while Walter Gretsch lasted longer, leaving in 1924 with a salesman colleague to establish Gretsch & Brenner, a small musical instrument importing company that lasted into the mid 1950s.

Meanwhile, Fred Sr. continued to expand the Gretsch company successfully in the early years of the 1900s. In 1916 construction was completed on a large ten-story building at 60 Broadway, Brooklyn, just over the Williamsburg Bridge that crosses the East River to connect Manhattan to Brooklyn in New York. This large, imposing building continued to house the factory and offices of the Fred Gretsch Mfg. Co. for many years.

By the early 1920s Gretsch was able to advertise to music dealers an enormous and flourishing line of instruments, primarily with the Rex and 20th Century brandnames and including banjos (the most popular stringed instrument of the time), mandolins, guitars, violins, band instruments, drums, bells, accordions, harmonicas, gramophones and a variety of accessories including strings, cases and stands.

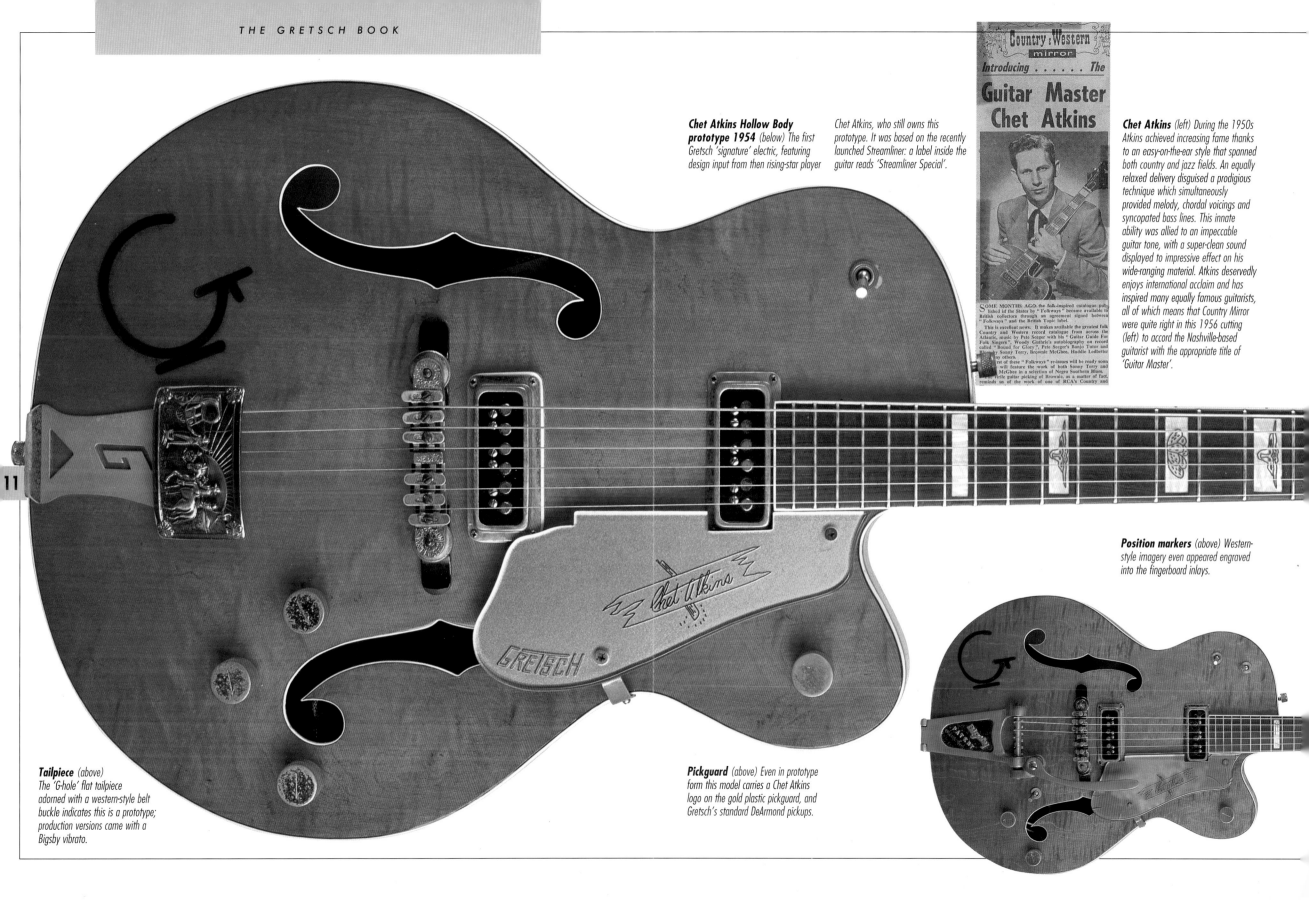

Chet Atkins Hollow Body prototype 1954 *(below) The first Gretsch 'signature' electric, featuring design input from then rising-star player*

Chet Atkins, who still owns this prototype. It was based on the recently launched Streamliner: a label inside the guitar reads 'Streamliner Special'.

Country & Western
mirror
Introducing . . . . . . The
Guitar Master
Chet Atkins

SOME MONTHS AGO, the folk-inspired catalogue published in the States by "Folkways" became available to British collectors through an agreement signed between "Folkways" and the British Topic label.
This is excellent news. It makes available the greatest folk Country and Western record catalogue from across the Atlantic, music by Pete Seeger with his "Guitar Guide For Folk Singers", Woody Guthrie's autobiography on record called "Bound for Glory", Pete Seeger's Banjo Tutor and records by Sonny Terry, Brownie McGhee, Huddie Ledbetter and many others.
Part of these "Folkways" re-issues will be ready soon and will feature the work of both Sonny Terry and Brownie McGhee in a selection of Negro Southern Blues. The virile guitar picking of Brownie, as a matter of fact, reminds us of the work of one of RCA's Country and

Chet Atkins *(left) During the 1950s Atkins achieved increasing fame thanks to an easy-on-the-ear style that spanned both country and jazz fields. An equally relaxed delivery disguised a prodigious technique which simultaneously provided melody, chordal voicings and syncopated bass lines. This innate ability was allied to an impeccable guitar tone, with a super-clean sound displayed to impressive effect on his wide-ranging material. Atkins deservedly enjoys international acclaim and has inspired many equally famous guitarists, all of which means that Country Mirror were quite right in this 1956 cutting (left) to accord the Nashville-based guitarist with the appropriate title of 'Guitar Master'.*

Position markers *(above) Western-style imagery even appeared engraved into the fingerboard inlays.*

Tailpiece *(above) The 'G-hole' flat tailpiece adorned with a western-style belt buckle indicates this is a prototype; production versions came with a Bigsby vibrato.*

Pickguard *(above) Even in prototype form this model carries a Chet Atkins logo on the gold plastic pickguard, and Gretsch's standard DeArmond pickups.*

11

Gretsch catalog 1950 (above) Inside is shown the sole Gretsch Spanish electric guitar of the time, the Electromatic Spanish.

Country Club 1956 (below) Introduced in 1954 and growing from the Electro II model, the Country Club became a mainstay model in the Gretsch line for 27 years. Although initially similar to its predecessor, the Country Club soon benefited from the color-conscious Gretsch treatment, effectively displayed by this example in a rare light/dark gray finish.

Corvette 1955 (above) This hollow body guitar succeeded the Electromatic Spanish in 1954 and, indicated by the continued use of the Electromatic logo on the headstock, it maintained the plain and simple theme of the earlier model, including basic hardware as well as a DeArmond single-coil pickup at the neck. On some examples the somewhat austere appearance was relieved by 'Jaguar Tan', to use Gretsch's term, a dark gold finish that aped Gibson's sole deviation from tradition on their gleaming Les Paul gold-top model and ES-295 of 1952.

Selector switch (below) The presence of a pickup selector switch here indicates a later example of this model.

Headstock (below) The Synchromatic logo was originally used on Gretsch's acoustic guitar models.

Spotlight on AL CAIOLA

Top CBS Guitarist Caiola, plays a heavy radio and TV schedule appearing with Archie Bleyer, Ray Bloch, Alfredo Antonini; records steadily as well. Al says the "Miracle Neck" of his Gretsch Electromatic Guitar (with twin Gretsch-DeArmond pickups) cuts down the tension of his heavy schedule, keeps his hands fresh for show-time: "Fastest, easiest-playing, richest-toned guitar I've ever owned." Write today for more about this sensational Gretsch innovation—plus the Gretsch Guitar Guide, yours FREE. Address: The Fred. Gretsch Mfg. Co., 60 Broadway, Brooklyn 11, N.Y. Dept. DB-402.

Al Caiola (above) Although better known for his later Epiphone 'signature' model, TV and movie session player Caiola was a Gretsch endorsee in the 1950s, here favoring an Electro II.

CONTROL NO. 5   CONTROL NO. 4

PICK-UP NO. 1

PICK-UP NO. 2

CONTROL NO. 1

CONTROL NO. 3

CONTROL NO. 2

Control No. 1 regulates volume of Pick-Up No. 1
Control No. 2 regulates volume of Pick-Up No. 2
Control No. 3 Bass-Treble Selector
Control No. 4 regulates volume of both Pick-Ups
Control No. 5 Pick-Up Selector

Melita bridge (above) From the early 1950s this complex-looking adjustable bridge began to appear on Gretsch guitars.

Electro II 1954 (above) One of Gretsch's first cutaway electric models, which evolved into the Country Club during 1954. Talented guitarist Jimmie Webster (left) worked for Gretsch and was responsible for many of the company's guitar designs and novel features. He is seen here playing his 'touch system' style on an Electro II.

Control layout (above) As Gretsch circuitry did not follow a conventional pattern, the company issued this informative leaflet in the 1950s.

Country Club 1955 (above) While Gretsch catered for tradition-based players by offering many models in sunburst or natural finishes, they also targeted the less conservative guitarist with more colorful hues. The dark 'Cadillac' green of this Country Club was a striking option, available from the model's launch in 1954 and further enhanced by gold-plated hardware.

Chet Atkins Hollow Body 1955
(left) This example displays all the classic Western features typical of an early first version of this model. Although initially considered somewhat over-the-top and soon abandoned, these aspects now contribute to make this one of the most desirable of all Gretsch guitars on the vintage market.

Chet Atkins Solid Body 1956
(right) This rather more compact semi-solid model partnered the Chet Atkins Hollow Body and of course bore more cowboy components. The Atkins connection distinguished it from Gretsch's slightly earlier Round Up model, another similarly countrified semi-solid, but Chet himself preferred to pick his Hollow Body.

13

Chet Atkins Strings (left) With Chet Atkins on board, Gretsch put his name on various companion products as well as the guitars, including strings and amplifiers. The strings were packaged in distinctive circular plastic boxes.

America's big favorite CHET ATKINS raves about his new Gretsch Guitars

Gretsch promos 1955 The catalog (below) introduced the Chet Atkins Hollow Body and Solid Body models in all their Western glory. Atkins (left) preferred the Hollow Body, but also advertised its semi-solid sibling.

Chet Atkins Hollow Body 1955
(above) Still owned by Chet Atkins, this is a very early production example of his namesake guitar, sent to him by

Gretsch. Note that the controls and six-saddle bridge are different from those seen on normal examples of the Hollow Body from a similar period.

At the end of the 1920s and into the early 1930s the guitar began to replace the banjo in general popularity as a more versatile and appealing instrument, and it was in about 1933 that Gretsch used its own name as a brand for guitars. The company offered a line of archtop acoustic instruments, the Gretsch American Orchestra series, as well as a number of flat-top acoustics such as the Gretsch Broadkaster. These guitars were not especially unusual or notable, although some later models in the acoustic line bore very distinctive cat's-eye and triangle shape soundholes.

Gretsch acoustics were offered alongside a still burgeoning wholesale list of other brandnames, including guitars from the 'big two' Chicago makers, Kay and Harmony. Gretsch also manufactured instruments for different outlets, including mail-order catalog companies such as Montgomery Ward and Sears, Roebuck. Altogether, the Gretsch operation supplied a multitude of musical lines including drums, guitars, banjos, mandolins... in fact virtually anything that might be played by the budding musician of the time.

Around 1930 Gretsch had spread their distribution network still wider across the US by opening a mid-western branch, in Chicago, headed up by Phil Nash. In combination with the New York factory and office this provided Gretsch with an efficient and profitable business throughout the United States: the New York office covered the area from the east coast to Ohio, the Chicago office from Ohio to the west coast.

ELECTROMATICALLY YOURS

The first 'Spanish' electric guitar bearing the Gretsch brand was offered by the company around 1939. Other than a scant description of this Electromatic Spanish model in a contemporary Gretsch catalog (but, alas, no photograph), little is known of the instrument. It certainly does not seem to have made much impact on the market – if indeed it was ever made in any quantity at all.

Electric guitars were still in their infancy and not yet well understood by makers or by players. Electric Hawaiian guitars had turned up earlier in the 1930s, and normal 'Spanish'

archtop acoustic guitars with built-in electric pickups and associated controls had been produced by makers such as Rickenbacker, National, Gibson and Epiphone at various times during the 1930s, but to little effect. With the United States' entry into World War II in 1942, Gretsch's Spanish electric slipped quietly from its apparent role as an unenthusiastic, doubtful experiment into non-existence.

Changes were happening elsewhere in the company. Fred Sr. was still nominally president of Gretsch, but in fact had effectively retired from active management in the early 1930s to devote himself entirely to the business he really loved, which was banking. He officially retired from Gretsch in 1942, and died ten years later. He was replaced as company president in '42 by his third son, William Walter Gretsch (generally known as Bill), who had taken over the Chicago office in the mid 1930s. Bill headed the Gretsch company until his premature death at the age of 44 in 1948. His brother Fred Gretsch Jr., already the company's treasurer, then took over as president. It would be Fred Jr. who would steer the company through the glory years in the 1950s and 1960s.

During World War II Gretsch continued to make some musical instruments but concentrated on government war contracts, manufacturing circular wooden hoops for use in gas-masks, for example. Of course, many Gretsch personnel were called up for active service, but the company was able to return to full instrument production during the years from 1946, and gradually re-organized into an outfit ready for the new challenges ahead in the 1950s.

LIFE AFTER WARTIME

Charles 'Duke' Kramer had started working for Gretsch's mid-western office in Chicago in 1935, first as a purchasing agent, later as a salesman. After a wartime stint in the army Kramer returned to his job with Gretsch in Chicago, taking over the running of the branch when Bill Gretsch died in 1948.

"When we all came back from the services," Kramer recalls, "we had a meeting in New York in 1946 to determine whether we wanted to continue as a jobber/distributor type operation, or whether we wanted to go major line and sell product under the Gretsch logo. Up to that time we had been making drums and guitars mostly for other people. So we decided we wanted to go major line. We couldn't do both immediately, so we started out in drums, and in 1947 and 1948 we introduced the Gretsch drum line. It was very shortly after that when we started to make our first electric model guitars."

Gretsch needed new people to promote these new lines, and hired Phil Grant to look after drums and Jimmie Webster for the guitar side. Grant was a professional drummer who played with the Pittsburgh Symphony Orchestra and the Edwin Franko Goldman band. Webster was a professional piano-tuner, pianist and guitarist – and, as we shall discover, he was to have far-reaching and profound influences on the development of Gretsch's electric guitar lines.

Grant recalls his first years at Gretsch and the changes happening to the business in the late 1940s: "The Gretsch company did carry on as a jobber – that is, a wholesaler who sells miscellaneous things to retail stores – and so that part of the business never really changed for us: Monopole band instruments, LaTosca accordions, Eagle strings, that kind of thing. It was just that on the drums and guitars we stopped selling to catalog houses and people like that who were only interested in low-price merchandise. We decided to go and shoot for the big stuff, and so the low-price items sort of faded into the background."

HARRY AND HIS BUILT-IN MIKE

Gretsch issued an 18-page brochure around 1950, *Your Gretsch Guitar Guide*, that underlined the company's new emphasis on guitars for professionals, and among other things publicized Gretsch's new and generous three-year guitar guarantee which covered any defects caused by faulty workmanship or defective materials. "The guitar you play is a definite factor in the quality of the music you produce," wrote Fred Gretsch Jr., adding with a final flourish: "and a Gretsch guitar truly glorifies the talents of the artist who commands it." Somewhat over the top, for sure, but it shows the direction in

which the company wanted to take the marketing of its new guitar models.

The first post-war electric guitar revived the Electromatic Spanish name, debuting in 1949 alongside a number of Synchromatic-series acoustic guitars. It had an archtop body with f-holes, at first finished in sunburst and later also available in natural. It had a single-coil pickup which the catalog described as a "built-in Gretsch mike", and it was made for Gretsch by Rowe Industries of Toledo, Ohio, a company run by Harry DeArmond. The pickup featured six individually adjustable polepieces in a distinctive black-topped chrome case. It was used by Gretsch until the late 1950s, and although in the 1951 catalog the unit was referred to as the Gretsch-DeArmond Fidelatone, a few years later the pickup officially received its more familiar name, the Gretsch Dynasonic; nonetheless, it remained a DeArmond-made item.

At $110 the 1949 Electromatic Spanish compared to similar rather basic instruments of the period such as Gibson's $137 ES-150 model. These were still non-cutaway guitars, and this body design already appeared old fashioned. Gibson had led the way in cutaway electrics with their ES-350 Premier model of 1947, and the wider acceptance of electric instruments was beginning to make a cutaway body a necessity. There was little point in playing high up the neck on an acoustic because the results were unlikely to be heard. It was wasted effort for the guitarist. But on an instrument equipped with a pickup and suitably amplified, a cutaway offered easier access to the now audible and musically useful upper reaches of the fingerboard.

So it was that Gretsch issued the Electromatic and Electro II cutaway-body electrics in 1951, and in effect proved that it really did take seriously the new electric guitar business. "Electric guitar at its peak!" proclaimed Gretsch of the twin-pickup $355 sunburst Electro II ($20 more for the natural version) complete with gold-plated hardware. Again, it was aimed to compete with the market leader, Gibson, whose comparable ES-350 was selling for $385 ($400 natural) in the early 1950s.

Gretsch's new electric cutaway models were first presented

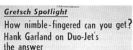

Hank "Sugar Foot" Garland and his Gretsch Guitar

Hank Garland (above) This talented
player later defected to Gibson but was
a Gretsch endorsee in the 1950s. Like
Chet Atkins, Garland embraced jazz and
country styles, and this perhaps explains
the Gretsch connection. He is cradling a
Duo Jet in this ad from the model's
launch year of 1953.

Controls (above) Many early Gretsch
electrics have a volume control for each
pickup and a master tone, plus separate
master volume and pickup selector.

Silver Jet 1955 (below) In 1954, a
year after the Duo Jet was launched,
Gretsch decided to enliven the model's
somewhat somber look by adding the
Silver Jet with a body front made from
the sparkle plastic material that the
company used on some of their drum
products. The chosen silver color
naturally proved to be effectively eye-
catching under stage (or bedroom)
lights, and was in pleasing contrast
to the body's black sides and back.

16

GRETSCH SOLID BODY TWIN PICKUP ELECTRIC GUITARS

Pickguard (above) The small, plain
plastic pickguard indicates an early
example of the Silver Jet.

Gretsch promo (right) Three semi-
solid models made a classy and colorful
debut in the company's impressive
catalog of 1955. From left to right they
are: the red Jet Fire Bird model; the
black Duo-Jet model; and the orange
Round Up model.

Position markers (below) Early Duo Jets have block fingerboard inlays.

Duo Jet 1955 (left) The Jet appeared in 1953 and was intended to gain some of the market held by Gibson's Les Paul guitar, launched the previous year. The similarities were obvious: both shared single-cutaway styling, a compact body design and two single-coil pickups. But Gretsch's semi-solid construction meant a noticeable reduction in overall weight, and the revised circuitry with master volume control on the cutaway yielded more subtle operation.

Jet Fire Bird 1960 (above) With red-fronted body, this model joined the semi-solid series in 1955. By 1960 it sported a zero fret (an extra fret next to the nut), 'half-moon' markers, Filter'Tron humbucker pickups, and revised circuitry. Bo Diddley (right) totes an earlier Bird plus an even louder jacket.

Jeff Beck's Duo Jet (above) Beck bought this '56 Jet as it was almost identical to the guitar used by his guitar hero Cliff Gallup of Gene Vincent's Blue Caps. Complete with DeArmonds and fixed-arm Bigsby, the guitar was acquired by Beck after recording his 'Crazy Legs' Gallup tribute LP of 1993.

to professional guitarists and music dealers at a three-day promotional show held at New York's Park Sheraton Hotel in January 1951. *The Music Trades* magazine reported that Gretsch's event enjoyed excellent attendance by "many top-flight guitarists" and dubbed it "an exciting forerunner of the important position the new Gretsch [models] will hold". Demonstrating the latest electrics as well as a number of acoustic models at the hotel launch was Jimmie Webster, described as Gretsch's "special representative".

WEBSTER'S GUITARAMA

Jimmie Webster was born in 1908 in Van Wert, Ohio, and later moved to Long Island, New York. He played piano and guitar and worked in the 1930s as a musician in New York City. He also made money as a qualified piano-tuner, and at one stage ran a music store, as did his piano-playing father, Harry. Webster's mother Kathryn also played and taught piano – sometimes when money was tight she had accompanied silent movies at the local cinema.

Webster had been casually involved with Gretsch before World War II, but it was in about 1946 that he began to work regularly for the company. His daughter, Jennifer Cohen, who was born in 1948, remembers: "He used to do so many things, and when I was growing up he started to work more for Gretsch. He began to travel a lot for them, promoting the guitars. I don't think he was ever exclusively a Gretsch employee, he just regularly billed them for his services, more like a freelance. He wanted to call his own shots and run his own life, and he always said he never wanted to be tied to them – that was his personality.

"So he worked several days of the week for Gretsch and on alternate days he tuned pianos: Monday, Wednesday, Friday he would go into Gretsch in Brooklyn, Tuesdays and Thursdays he would tune pianos around the small town we lived in on Long Island. He was very much in demand as a piano tuner, very popular." He seems to have been popular with his colleagues at Gretsch, too. Phil Grant's comment – "Jimmie was a wonderful guy, and very smart" – is typical.

As we shall see, Webster became Gretsch's main ideas man, bombarding management and production teams with all manner of guitar models and add-on gadgets in an effort to distinguish Gretsch's instruments from the growing competition. Webster would also travel around the US, and occasionally abroad, to promote the latest items at trade fairs and in live public shows that became known as Gretsch 'Guitaramas'. Webster was a great find for Gretsch: a musician, an inventor and a salesman, all wrapped up in one likable, outgoing personality. He probably did more than anyone else to spread the word about Gretsch guitars, and became a traveling ambassador for Gretsch, for electric guitars, and for guitar playing in general.

TAPPING INTO THE TOUCH SYSTEM

Webster's own playing style was unusual, and the company made a plus of this too, often using space in catalogs and brochures to explain about the 'Touch System'. This was also a specific peg on which Gretsch could artfully hang general publicity for its guitars: a 1952 ad, for example, mentions appearances by Webster showing off "his amazing Touch System of guitar playing" on a couple of TV shows.

What was the Touch System? Modern readers will probably be familiar with the 'tapping' technique that Eddie Van Halen did much to popularize in the 1980s, or even the more concerted if less commercially successful efforts of Stanley Jordan. In fact Jimmie Webster began to use a similar idea back in the 1940s. He would produce chordal rhythms with his left hand using a sort of rapid hammering-on motion and, without a pick, simultaneously play the melody by tapping the strings against the upper fingerboard with his right-hand fingers, adding a bassline with his thumb. "It's like patting your head and rubbing your stomach at the same time," Webster joked once with an interviewer. (There's a photo of Webster playing in the style on page 9.)

Webster's use of the Touch System probably had quite a lot to do with the fact that he was originally a piano player – in fact more than one observer has told us that Webster was a better pianist than guitarist. Presumably it seemed natural when he played guitar to use both hands in a similar manner to the way he would on piano. Many people who heard him play say that at first they couldn't believe that all the sounds were coming from one person playing one guitar, that it seemed like at least two guitarists.

"Credit for the discovery of the Touch System belongs to Harry DeArmond," admitted Webster in a 1950 Gretsch brochure, "whose name you probably recognize since he manufactures the popular and powerful DeArmond pickups." It's been suggested that DeArmond developed the system to demonstrate his pickups (which of course Gretsch used on their electric guitars at the time). Webster continued: "Professionals like the Touch System because it gives them a whole new field of solo possibilities. People who play for their own amusement and for their friends find the guitar now more complete within itself than ever before." Unfortunately this was rather optimistic as the style did not catch on at the time, although Webster happily and effectively continued to use it for decades. It wasn't until Van Halen's high-volume application of a similar concept in the 1980s – by which time Webster had been dead for a number of years – that tapping techniques really took off.

SOLID OUTRAGE

During the first few years of the 1950s Gretsch was content to offer a selection of four electric archtop models, but was no doubt keeping an eye on moves being made by other manufacturers toward the development of a solidbody electric instrument. During 1950 Fender in California had been the first to bring a commercial product of this type to the marketplace. Gretsch certainly noticed this, because Fender called its new solidbody electric the Broadcaster, a name that Gretsch still used (but spelled Broadkaster) for a number of its drum kits and individual drum products.

Fender salesman Dale Hyatt remembers the reaction from Gretsch: "There was a camaraderie between the manufacturers in the early days and no one was trying to beat the other to a patent or anything like that. So Gretsch just pointed it out and we agreed to change it." Thus, at Gretsch's request, Fender dropped the name of its innovative Broadcaster, which from 1951 became the Fender Telecaster. At first most guitar makers considered this solidbody a small-fry manufacturer's oddity which probably would not last. But attitudes changed relatively quickly.

Gretsch was certainly surprised when it saw its chief rival Gibson produce a solidbody electric guitar in 1952, the Gibson Les Paul model. Ted McCarty, Gibson's president from 1950 to 1966, remembers that Fred Gretsch Jr. was amazed that such a traditional company should become involved in this modern nonsense. "When we introduced the Les Paul at the trade show," McCarty recalls, "Fred Gretsch, who was a personal friend of mine, said, 'How could you do this? Why and how could you do that for Gibson?' We were good friends, and I said, 'Fred, somebody's got to stop this guy Fender, he's just about trying to take over.' Fred said, 'But Ted, anybody with a band-saw and a router can make a solidbody guitar, and I just can't believe that Gibson would do it.'"

Fred Jr. overcame his initial outrage and, seeing that Fender and Gibson were actually beginning to *sell* these new-style electrics, the businessman in him took over. In 1953 Gretsch launched its first solidbody, the $230 Duo Jet. Well, at least it had the *look* of a solid... and especially recalled the general outline and look of the $225 Gibson Les Paul.

At the time, Gibson used a solid sandwich of mahogany and maple, Fender used solid ash... but Gretsch assembled the body of the Duo Jet from separate pieces of mahogany that incorporated many routed channels and pockets for cables and components, to which it would then add a pressed arched top. (Production manager Bill Hagner, who had joined Gretsch in 1941, says that a good deal of Gretsch's raw and processed timber for guitars and drums was supplied by Jasper Wood Products of Jasper, Indiana.) In fact the best description of Gretsch's new solid guitar is probably 'semi-solid'. But in terms of its look, function, catalog description and intended place in the market, the Duo Jet was in effect Gretsch's first solidbody

Eddy's paperwork (right) With a thoroughness untypical of many famous guitarists, Duane Eddy has retained the original guarantee and sales contract for his Chet Atkins Hollow Body. The bank sales contract (right) is signed by Duane's father Lloyd and records a purchase from Ziggie's in Phoenix, Arizona, for $420 spread over 24 months, starting on October 21st 1957. This guitar has certainly appreciated in value!

Loving care (above) The fine condition of this well-used guitar reflects Duane Eddy's fondness for his number one instrument.

Bridge (above) Duane Eddy's famous Gretsch is still all-original, including the single-saddle 'bar' bridge.

Duane Eddy's Chet Atkins Hollow Body 1957 (above) Duane Eddy used this instrument on many of his instrumental hits from the 1950s onwards. He favored playing the melody line on the lower strings, and this became a sonic trademark, aided by his trusty Gretsch. The guitar played a significant part in the creation of Eddy's signature 'twangy' tone, a deep and dark sound very different to that employed by Chet Atkins.

Eddie Cochran (left) Another famous player of the Chet Atkins Hollow Body, Cochran swapped the neck-position DeArmond pickup for a Gibson P90, as this 1983 Guitar Player cover shows.

Chet Atkins Hollow Body 1958
(below) The late 1950s brought numerous changes to Gretsch electric models, including the Hollow Body. The 1958 example shown here displays little of the overt Western decoration found on earlier versions, and sports half-moon fingerboard position markers, Filter'Tron humbuckers and accompanying two-switch tone circuitry.

Chet Atkins sleeve 1961 (left) Naturally Gretsches often featured prominently on Atkins' album sleeves, and this Christmas LP is no exception, complete with a frosty Hollow Body.

Headstock (below) Note the horseshoe inlay, which replaced the original steer head logo in 1956.

21

Duane Eddy on stage (left) Around October 1957 a youthful Duane Eddy proudly displays his prized new Chet Atkins Hollow Body, although its orange splendor is in imminent danger of being eclipsed by a somewhat showstopping shirt. Perhaps it is for the best that this photo, from Duane's personal archive, is in restful black and white. Eddy moved from his first electric guitar, a Gibson Les Paul gold-top, to the new Gretsch — he particularly wanted a guitar with a Bigsby vibrato — and went on to use it successfully both in the studio and on stage. After a dalliance with a 'signature' Guild model during the 1960s, he returned to the Gretsch with which he had become so strongly identified in sight and sound through many hit tours and records.

Neo-Classic fingerboard (above) Gretsch piled on the hyperbole in this late 1950s leaflet extolling the virtues of their new 'Neo-Classic' fingerboard. Behind the marketing hype was a length of quite normal ebony (later rosewood) carrying those distinctive half-moon-shaped position markers, located at the edge of the board to ensure "no obstructions to mar your playing" and a "smooth playing surface the entire length of fingerboard". This was a lot of fuss over a piece of wood... but it made for interesting if not necessarily informative reading.

electric guitar, as Duke Kramer confirms: "A lot of people called it a semi-solid, because we routed out an awful lot of space in the wood for the electronics, but basically we considered it a solidbody guitar."

Unusually, the new Duo Jet had in its early years a body front covered in a black plastic material, as used on some Gretsch drums. The Jet's control layout emphasized the start of Gretsch's predilection for positioning a master volume knob on the cutaway bout (the Electro II gained one around the same time), and the model carried Gretsch's unique two-piece strap buttons, one part of which was screwed into the body so that the hole in the strap could be placed over the protruding threaded spigot. A knurled knob was then screwed down to hold the strap securely in place – an early take on the idea of locking strap buttons. The Jet also featured the Melita Synchro-Sonic bridge, which had been a feature of some Gretsch electrics since the previous year.

INSTANT MELITA

The Synchro-Sonic was the first guitar bridge to offer independent intonation adjustment for each string – it beat Gibson's Tune-O-Matic version by at least a year. The design was brought to Gretsch by Sebastiano ('Johnny') Melita, who subsequently manufactured the units for them in his own workshops. It's an apparently complex mass of chrome-plated metal that looks as if it might be more at home on a saxophone (see, for example, the one fitted to the Electro II on page 9), but Gretsch immediately recognized the Melita's potential to provide the more accurate intonation that was required on electric guitars. Loosening one of the easily accessible row of six top-mounted screws allows the attached saddle to be moved back or forward in order to set optimum intonation for that string. In a June 1952 ad Gretsch promoted the Melita as "for the first time" offering "perfect tuning and clearer high notes" thanks to its "separate adjustable saddle for each string [which] permits split-hair tuning."

Two further solidbody models in the style of the Duo Jet were added to the line in 1954: the country-flavored Round Up; and the sparkle-finished Silver Jet. Country & Western music was spreading in popularity – artists like Hank Williams even had hits on the pop charts in 1953 – and Gretsch aimed the Round Up squarely at the rising number of country players by adorning their guitar with unrelenting Western decoration.

DRUMMING UP A SPARKLE TOP

The Round Up had a steer's head logo on the headstock and pickguard. There were various Western motifs (mostly steer's heads and cacti) engraved into the block fingerboard markers. A belt buckle with a homely wagon-train scene was attached to the tailpiece. There was even a big G (for Gretsch) actually branded into the front of the 'Western' orange-finish body, which had metal-studded leather stuck around its sides embossed with yet more cacti and steer's heads. And to hang all this from the shoulders of the adoring new owner, the guitar came with a leather strap encrusted with rhinestones and decked out with the obligatory steers and cacti. Subtle it was not. Gretsch optimistically described the Round Up as having "masculine beauty".

Equally unsubtle was the Silver Jet, also launched in 1954, which came with a silver sparkle finish on the body front, this time more obviously a product of Gretsch's drum department. Phil Grant remembers how it came about: "We used drum covering on some guitars, and that was Jimmie Webster's idea. We would buy our plain, pearl and sparkle drum covering in plastic sheets from a local company called Monsanto, and Jimmie went into the factory one day and could see we were making drums with it. He said, 'Well, why can't we make guitars with it?' So we did! We would glue the plastic covering to the body, just like you do on a drum shell. Maybe the acceptance wasn't 100 per cent out there in the field, but they were good looking guitars."

In what was a busy year for the inventive guitar department, Gretsch also revised their archtop electrics. The non-cutaway Electro II was dropped, while the three other models were renamed: the non-cutaway Electromatic Spanish became the Corvette; the Electromatic became the Streamliner; and the cutaway Electro II became the Country Club. Most guitar makers admit to having a hard time when it comes to thinking up model names, and Gretsch was doubtless no exception. But it's unusual to reveal the thought process in public; even so, Gretsch prematurely announced the renamed Electro II as the 'Country Song' guitar in an October 1953 ad. In fact, when the properly retitled Country Club appeared in 1954 it heralded the start of a 27-year run that would make it the longest-lived model name in Gretsch's history.

Cadillac Green or Jaguar Tan?

Another significant addition to the Gretsch line in 1954 was the option of colored finishes for some models, beyond the normal sunburst or natural varieties. We've already noted the company's use of drum coverings on the Silver Jet and the black Duo Jet, but equally flamboyant paint finishes were on the way. Automobile marketing was having a growing influence on guitar manufacturers in the early 1950s, and the theme was especially evident in Gretsch's colorful campaign of 1954, with a 'Cadillac Green' option for the Country Club and a 'Jaguar Tan' (actually a dark gold) for the Streamliner. The paints came from DuPont, who also supplied most of the car companies (and later Fender too). Gretsch also drew again on its experience in finishing and lacquering drums in different colors, applying know-how that already existed within the company to help its guitars stand out in the marketplace.

There were isolated precedents for colored guitars – Gibson's gold ES-295 and Les Paul of 1952, Fender's infrequent and as-yet unofficial custom colors – but for a few years Gretsch made the use of color into a marketing bonus almost entirely its own. Through the middle 1950s it also added a number of pleasant two-tone options – yellows, coppers, ivories – contrasting a darker body back and sides against a lighter-colored body front (see page 24/25 for examples), and this was yet another idea that came from long-standing techniques used in Gretsch's drum department. With an eye on the TV boom of the 1950s, Gretsch's vice-president Emerson Strong told a reporter: "These color combinations are likely to become even more effective as color television receivers are installed and the public grows increasingly accustomed to the bright hues they will see on their screens every day."

By October 1954, Gretsch's guitar pricelist could boast a respectable line-up of six electric guitars. There were three archtops: the Corvette at $137.50 (in sunburst; a natural option cost $147.50); Streamliner at $225 (sunburst; Jaguar Tan at $235; natural $245); and Country Club $375 (sunburst; Cadillac Green $385; natural $395); plus three solidbodys: the Duo Jet at $230 (with four-string baritone ukulele and tenor guitar options listed at the same price); Silver Jet $230; and Round Up $300.

Al, Mary, Hank and Chet

The success of Gibson's Les Paul guitar – well over 2000 were sold in 1953 alone – alerted other manufacturers, including Gretsch, to the value of a 'signature' model endorsed by a famous player. Today the practice is very familiar, but back in the 1950s it was a new, exciting and potentially profitable area of musical instrument marketing.

A signature guitar named for a musician was a step beyond the kind of advertising that Gretsch already ran which merely highlighted the use of its guitars by particular players. Gretsch's ad agency of the time, the New York-based Mitchell Morrison, devised a series of 'Gretsch Spotlight' ads that appeared in musicians' publications and trade magazines in the early 1950s, featuring mainly jazz and studio guitarists such as Al Caiola (with an Electro II), Mary Osborne (with a Country Club) and Hank Garland (with a Duo Jet).

Phil Grant acted as a liaison between Gretsch, Mitchell Morrison and the musicians, and remembers the process well: "Everybody liked a little publicity, they figured it would help them with their career: your name and picture in the papers. But to be honest Al Caiola had a limited following, he would only be known to studio musicians, and Mary Osborne was pretty much the same, though of course she had the glamour angle. Really those ads didn't have much impact, they were just a name and a picture."

Streamliner 1957 (right)
The Streamliner succeeded the Electromatic in 1954, but until 1958 the headstock continued to carry the Electromatic logo, as on this example. Note also the hump-top-block position markers, introduced in 1955. Unlike its predecessor, the Streamliner also came in colors, such as the yellow/brown combination pictured.

"Get fast, positive sound"

SAL SALVADOR ON GUITARS

Praises quick responsive action of his Gretsch guitar . . . calls tone quality the finest. Likes slim neck and streamlined Gretsch body . . . says his Gretsch guitar "feels comfortable—plays fastest".

Sal plays the Gretsch Electromatic Cutaway model . . . used it for his new record album "Frivolous Sal" (Bethlehem—BCP 59).

Top Jazz stylists play Gretsch guitars—why don't you? See your dealer . . . write for Free Gretsch guitar catalog . . . many popular models shown in color.

GRETSCH The FRED. GRETSCH Mfg. Co., Dept. HB56 60 Broadway, Brooklyn 11, N. Y.

Convertible 1957 (right) Another colorful model, here a cream and brown two-toner. Pickup and controls were fixed to the pickguard, not the body top, allowing the latter to vibrate freely, improving resonance, and the guitar was thus a 'proper' acoustic as well as an electric — hence the title. In 1959 it was renamed the Sal Salvador for its best-known exponent; jazzman Salvador is seen (above) in a 1956 ad .

INSPIRED BY THE FAMOUS FAST-ACTION, FASHION-WISE CAR . . .

THE NEW GRETSCH "STREAMLINER" GUITAR IN

Jaguar Tan

THE FRED. GRETSCH MFG CO

Streamliner 1955 (left) Block position markers indicate an early example, finished in the all-gold color option that Gretsch called Jaguar Tan, a choice emphasized in promotion for the new guitar (above). The 1955 ad claims auto inspiration, but maybe Gibson's gold was a stronger influence.

24

Clipper 1957 (left) Gretsch's cheaper models often have dot fingerboard markers. The Clipper, originally a non-cutaway model, gained a single cutaway in 1957, and this example is in a cream/gray two-tone, rarer than the usual sunburst or natural finishes.

White Falcon 1955 (right) Formerly the property of Brian Setzer, this is an early example of Gretsch's upscale extravagance. Although still over-endowed with kitsch opulence (and this example has extra headstock decoration), it exudes a degree of quiet class compared to the knob-festooned feathered brethren that followed. And while the white finish has, as so often, faded to cream, this guitar still has a clean air — somewhat at odds with the abundance of gold sparkle plastic.

Birth of the Falcon? (below) During World War II Jimmie Webster sent home a cutting from a services newspaper showing him performing in an Army Air Corps theater production. On the reverse of the cutting is the paper's name: The White Falcon. Could this be the source of Webster's inspiration for the name of the deluxe guitar he later designed for Gretsch?

First flight (above) Jimmie Webster, the man responsible for designing the White Falcon, pictured demoing an experimental early version (note black pickguard) at the Gretsch 'Guitarama' show in New York in March 1954, assisted by Gretsch's vice-president in charge of the company's New York base, Phil Grant.

25

What Gretsch needed was its own Les Paul; in other words, a generally well known player whose name it could put on an instrument and use to attract fresh, untapped interest in its guitars. Around 1954, Jimmie Webster came up with the answer: Chet Atkins. It was a solution that in time would completely turn around Gretsch's fortunes.

In the mid 1950s Atkins was making his mark as a talented Nashville-based country guitarist. "I was already doing well when Gretsch approached me," recalls Atkins. "I was on the Grand Ole Opry, I was playing on the network [radio] shows, and I think I was already on national television then, Jimmy Dean had a show on CBS and he'd have me on every once in a while. I was pretty popular nationally when I went with Gretsch," Atkins concludes.

He remembers Jimmie Webster contacting him in Nashville, at a time when Atkins was using a D'Angelico Excel acoustic cutaway archtop into which he'd installed a Gibson pickup. "I had seen people playing Gretsch guitars, a couple of my friends played them," says Atkins. "Then Jimmie Webster would come to town to demonstrate Gretsch guitars, and he wanted me to play them. They had some design, but I didn't like it. But he kept after me, I remember once he took me over to a music store to try some things – he really wanted me to play one of their guitars. So finally he said, 'Well, why don't you design one that you would like?' And with that, Jimmie invited me out to the factory in New York."

The suggestion interested Atkins, and he made some preliminary inquiries. "Les Paul had his endorsement with Gibson and so I called him – he and my brother Jimmy had worked together in a trio. I said to Les, 'How much royalties should I get?' He hummed and hawed around, finally gave me a number, don't know if it was right or not. Then someone else said to me, 'Why don't you get a lawyer to go with you?' But I didn't do that, I was afraid a lawyer'd queer the deal by asking too much or something. When you're young like that, money doesn't matter."

An insider remembers the deliberations that also went on at Gretsch concerning the deal: "When Jimmie Webster first mentioned that he ought to get someone like Chet Atkins to endorse the guitar, Mr. Gretsch said, 'Why should I pay a hillbilly guitar player to use his name on our guitars?'" But Webster obviously managed to persuade Fred Jr. of the advantages. Fred was later able to write to his dealers: "Sell young people on a *desire* to play a Gretsch instrument... the confidence, so important to youngsters, of being able to say, 'Now I own a Chet Atkins guitar.'"

Soon after the suggestion from Webster, Atkins flew up from Nashville to New York for a meeting at Gretsch. "I went over to Brooklyn to the factory," recalls Atkins, "and visited with Mr. Gretsch and Emerson Strong, Jimmie Webster and Phil Grant. They were very nice, and we came up with the design for the orange Gretsch Chet Atkins. I think if Jimmie Webster were alive today he would tell you that the most important thing he ever did was to sign me to Gretsch, because they started selling the hell out of guitars."

ATKINS IN 'WESTERN JUNK' SHOCK

You can see the prototype for the Chet Atkins Hollow Body model pictured on page 11, made probably in 1954 and before its name had even been finalized. The label inside calls it a 'Streamliner Special'. "That's the first one I received," Atkins explains. "They sent it to me and said, 'How about this?' But I wanted a Bigsby vibrato on it, and I especially didn't like the f-holes, and later on we changed those. They also put all this junk on it, the cattle and the cactus, which didn't appeal to me at all."

Gretsch had reckoned that with Chet's country connections there was an opportunity to use again the Western decorations they'd devised for their Round Up guitar. As Duke Kramer puts it: "Instead of giving a pair of cowboy boots with every guitar, we put this Western stuff on it." Despite his strong reservations about the Western paraphernalia, Atkins gave in. "I was so anxious to get my name on a guitar, so I said oh... that's fine. I was *thrilled* to have my name on a guitar like Les Paul had his name on the Gibson. At the time I was full of ambition and I wanted to be known all over the world as a great guitarist, and that was one brick in the edifice that would help that happen."

In fact, the Western decorations were gradually removed from the original Chet Atkins models over the following years. Gretsch also gave ground by adding a Bigsby vibrato to the production model, in line with Atkins' request. And as well as the Hollow Body model it offered the Chet Atkins Solid Body, essentially a Round Up with a Bigsby vibrato replacing the belt-buckle tailpiece – and, despite the name, the Solid Body had Gretsch's customary semi-solid construction.

The two new models were announced, still with a hazy approach to the model names, in the December 1954 issue of *The Music Trades*, under the heading Gretsch To Have New Guitars, Chet Atkins Country Style. "Chet Atkins, top favorite of the Grand Ole Opry and one of the nation's best guitarists, plays and endorses the new Gretsch 'Chet Atkins Country' model guitar. Chet Atkins Country Style Electromatic guitars are available in the conventional hollow body or the solid body. Both have Gretsch DeArmond built-in pickups, slim, fast playing Miracle Neck and built-in vibrola. Both models will be available for delivery after January 1, 1955, and are priced at $360 list (case extra)."

Atkins had little to do with the Solid Body model, and it's described by one Gretsch staffer as a "mistake"; it was dropped after a few years. The Hollow Body, however, became Atkins' exclusive instrument for his increasingly popular work.

In reality there is very often a divide between what a guitar company sees as right for the market and what the endorsing player requires personally from an instrument. Les Paul, for example, would invariably modify his namesake models that Gibson supplied to him. Chet Atkins, reflecting now on his original Gretsch guitars of the mid 1950s, remembers that he wasn't entirely happy with what he was given: "I played that orange Gretsch Hollow Body guitar, but I hated the sound of the pickups at first," he recalls of the DeArmond units. "The magnets pulled so strong on the strings that there was no sustain there, especially on the bass." He would have to wait until 1958 for a change in that department.

Meanwhile, Gretsch was happy to see the effect that its new endorsement deal was having. The 1955 catalog trumpeted: "Every Chet Atkins appearance, whether in person or on TV... and every new album he cuts for RCA Victor, wins new admirers to swell the vast army of Chet Atkins fans." Phil Grant, Gretsch vice-president at the time, says: "I think the following that Chet had in country music surpassed even Les Paul's general following. You can't undervalue Chet's importance – he was the greatest thing that ever happened to us." Speaking about the original Hollow Body as well as the later Chet Atkins guitars, he adds succinctly and accurately: "The Gretsch Chet Atkins models put us on the map."

MODERN FALCONRY

Not content with the coup of attracting Chet Atkins to the company, Jimmie Webster was also experimenting during 1954 with some ideas for a guitar that would become Gretsch's top-of-the-line model. "I have a feeling the White Falcon was his dream guitar," says Webster's daughter Jennifer, "and I remember when he was developing it there was talk that this was going to be something real special."

Special it certainly was. The White Falcon was first marketed by Gretsch in 1955, and it was an overwhelmingly impressive instrument. The cutaway archtop hollow body was finished in a gleaming white paint finish, as was the new 'winged' design headstock, and both bore gold sparkle decorations again borrowed from the Gretsch drum department. All the metalwork was gold-plated, including the Grover 'stair-step' Imperial tuners and the stylish new tailpiece (since nicknamed the 'Cadillac' because of its use of a V-shaped element similar to the car company's logo). The fingerboard markers had suitably ornithoid engravings, and the gold plastic pickguard featured a flying falcon about to land on the nearby Gretsch logo. It was, simply, a stunner.

"Cost was never considered in the planning of this guitar," boasted the Gretsch publicity. "We were planning an instrument for the artist-player whose caliber justifies and demands the utmost in striking beauty, luxurious styling, and peak tonal performance and who is willing to pay the price." To

Body binding The all-white body of the Penguin was bound with contrasting gold sparkle plastic.

Pickguard (above) Just as the White Falcon had a pickguard depicting the sleek, majestic bird, so the White Penguin has... a penguin.

Tailpiece (above) This model employs a tubular frame-type tailpiece with 'G' logo, often nicknamed the 'Cadillac'.

White Penguin 1958 (right) This later example displays the changes that affected all the semi-solids and many other electrics in the Gretsch line around 1958. The bound ebony fingerboard now carries half-moon markers instead of engraved hump-top blocks; the DeArmond single-coil pickups have given way to Filter'Tron humbuckers; and the normal rotary tone control has been replaced by a switch relocated alongside the pickup selector. On this particular guitar the plastic pickguard has suffered the ravages of time, with a break near the neck pickup, a common fate to befall this brittle material.

White Penguin 1956 (below) This compact alternative to the White Falcon, also introduced in 1955, is now considered one of the rarest and most desirable of Gretsch guitars. Despite its comical name, the Penguin adopted the same upscale appointments as the more dignified Falcon, including an ebony fingerboard with engraved markers, gold plating, Melita bridge, bejeweled knobs and plenty of gold sparkle plastic. Beneath the glitz lurked standard Duo Jet specs, with normal circuit and DeArmond pickups.

Headstock (below) The headstock duplicates that of the Falcon, complete with 'winged' vertical Gretsch logo.

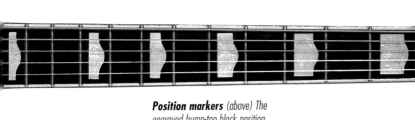

Position markers (above) The engraved hump-top block position markers indicate a pre-1958 example.

White Falcon 1959 (below) By the late 1950s Gretsch's flagship electric had incorporated many of the changes made to its lesser companions. This example has half-moon markers, Filter'Tron humbuckers and revised circuitry. The headstock carries the normal 'T-roof' logo and a nameplate, and a Space Control bridge replaces the Melita type.

29

Gretsch catalog 1961 (above) The cover displays a pair of White Falcons: the standard model surmounts a post-'59 stereo version with distinctive four-plus-one switch layout.

In a typical Gretsch touch, these top-of-the-line guitars are not pictured inside the '61 catalog, only on the cover. And each guitar has a different number of frets – a typical Gretsch quirk.

be precise, $600. The next highest in the line at the time was a $400 Country Club. Gibson's most expensive archtop electric in 1955 was the $690 Super 400CESN – but by comparison that was a sedate, natural-finish product of the more conventional Kalamazoo-based company. Meanwhile, over in New York, Gretsch proclaimed the idiosyncratic White Falcon as "the finest guitar we know how to make – and what a beauty!"

For Jimmie Webster, a white guitar was not such a new idea. His daughter Jennifer has a picture of her father playing in his Army Air Corps band during World War II, and he's using a Harmony guitar that clearly bears a white finish. Even more intriguing among Jennifer Cohen's collection of memorabilia is a 1943 newspaper cutting sent home by Jimmie during the war (it's pictured on page 25). "He's mentioned in the article, and there's a little arrow pointing to 'me'," she laughs. "Then if you flip it over, you can see that this forces newspaper is called *The White Falcon*. I really think that's where the name for the guitar came from."

FLIGHT OF THE BIG WHITE BIRD

Another influence on the style of the White Falcon may have come from the banjos that Gretsch marketed (for example, it had acquired the Bacon & Day banjo company in the late 1930s). Some of its more ostentatious banjos would use gold trim, fancy fingerboard markers and rhinestone inlays. It's fair to deduce that features of the White Falcon such as its distinctive jeweled knobs and feathery fingerboard inlays may well have been inspired by Gretsch's banjos. There's no reason to suppose that the borrowings would be limited to the drum department, and Jimmie Webster was probably fond of wandering around the entire factory and warehouse in his search for new ideas.

"We were always looking for something new to bring out at the NAMM conventions," says Duke Kramer of the White Falcon. At these important regular gatherings of the National Association of Music Merchants the major manufacturers would show their new models, usually in advance of appearing on the market, and dealers would visit from all over the

country to decide which of the new wares they would eventually want to stock in their stores.

An early White Falcon prototype had been displayed at one of Gretsch's own local promotional events in March 1954, but the guitar's first big showing was at the major NAMM show in Chicago four months later. Gretsch enticed dealers by billing the still experimental Falcon as one of its 'Guitars Of The Future' (along with the green Country Club and tan Streamliner).

"We followed the automobile industry," explains Kramer. "General Motors had what they called the Autorama show where they would display a dreamlike, futuristic car model. We felt, well... we could do that on a guitar. So we made the White Falcon for the show. It created quite a stir. We had it on a turntable with spotlights on it and it looked very special. Because of the response at that show, Fred was forced to go into production on the Falcon – which he didn't want to do, because it's a miserable guitar to have to make!"

Phil Grant also remembers the Falcon's reception among the music store owners, and how this flagship model became a help to Gretsch's general marketing efforts. "Our sales force always had a struggle getting our guitars accepted, because Gibson were number one," he says. "So if Gibson had one dealer in a city, we had to look to find a dealer that wasn't quite as hip and quite as knowledgeable to put our guitars in. And of course the best dealers in town would obviously have Gibson. It became easier when Jimmie Webster got the thing going and we had the White Falcon and guitars like that. The dealers were getting calls for the Falcon, and when that happens they're a little more agreeable to putting in stock."

Gretsch probably began to supply dealers with the first Falcons in 1955, and the influence of this spectacular new model even spread to other guitar manufacturers. Don Randall, head of Fender Sales at the time, says that Gretsch's colored guitars influenced Fender to officially offer in 1956 its 'player's choice' color options (known from the following year as 'custom colors').

"I was out in the field and sales oriented," explains Randall,

30

Twin cutaways (below) The double-cut Falcon came in 1962, a style following Gibson's fashion lead.

All his own work (right) This picture from the collection of Jimmie Webster's daughter Jennifer shows her pipe-smoking father in about 1962 wielding a single-cutaway White Falcon Stereo. It's equipped with the 'second-version' stereo's four-plus-one selector layout, as well as double string dampers with associated controls — all products of the fertile Webster brain. Unusually, this non-vibrato example also carries a 'Tone Twister', the small device that can be seen attached to the strings just in front of the tailpiece. Exerting force on the short, flat arm caused a slight degree of desirable pitch change — plus a severe risk of unwanted string breakage. Gretsch fitted this unfriendly thing to various cheaper models, but its presence on this White Falcon would suggest that it was a guitar meant only for the expert hands of its creator.

Jimmie Webster's White Falcon Stereo 1966 (left) As originator of the White Falcon and Gretsch's chief demonstrator, Jimmie Webster used many examples of the company's top guitar through the years. This 1966 example displays a gamut of guitar gadgets conceived by the inventive Webster, whose experimentation would constantly yield new ideas, many of which found their way to production models, and often to a mixed reaction. Here, offset position dots at the top of the fingerboard signify the 'T Zone Tempered Treble' angled frets, meant to offer improved intonation. A standby switch is added to the two-volume/five-selector stereo layout, while double string dampers (behind the back pickup) add two lever controls either side of the bridge, and the vibrato tailpiece has a telescopic adjustable arm. Located in front of the bridge is the 'Floating Sound' unit, a bar-frame device through which the strings pass; based on the principle of the tuning fork, it was supposed to enhance tone and increase sustain.

Gretsch catalog 1961 (above) The cheaper Anniversary also got the stereo treatment, this time splitting single-coil pickups to two amps.

Vibrato tailpiece (above) This version features a telescopic arm which allows adjustment of its overall length.

33

Jimmie Webster (left) Stereo guitar was another idea developed for Gretsch by Jimmie Webster. He was a keen advocate, too, demoing an early White Falcon Stereo to Chet Atkins at the New York Gretsch Guitarama in October 1958 (far left) and promoting the concept with his 'Unabridged' album (left) which he recorded on a Falcon Stereo two months later.

White Falcon Stereo 1958 (above) The first type of stereo model can be spotted by the pickups. They are positioned closer together than normal, and often have fewer than the usual number of polepieces on each unit.

Country Club Stereo 1958 (below) The Club also came as a stereo version; this green example has the first-version layout of close-spaced pickups with fewer polepieces. On Gretsch's later stereo guitars the humbuckers were spaced normally and a revised circuitry was developed that had a multi-switch control system.

Chet Atkins Hollow Body custom (left) This unusual black guitar was originally owned by Chet Atkins, who gave it to RCA engineer Bill Porter. Ray Butts, better known for designing Gretsch's Filter'Tron humbuckers, put pickup polepieces in the end of the fingerboard to help Atkins' experiments in isolating the fifth and sixth strings for electronic octave effects. Another departure from the normal Hollow Body is the pair of gold sparkle fake f-holes.

Ray Butts' Silver Jet testbed (right) Gretsch supplied Ray Butts with this unfinished Silver Jet in the late 1950s to enable him to carry out experimental work on pickups and circuitry. As usual in engineering practicality has taken precedence over appearance, and the large, ungainly looking board attached to the front enabled components to be changed easily. (See also back view, pictured top right.) This testbed was used to develop Gretsch's stereo guitar system, with Butts' solid technical knowledge backing up Jimmie Webster's continuing stream of ideas.

Silver Jet experimental pickup (above) Ray Butts has modified the Filter'Tron humbucker pickup on this Silver Jet to provide split outputs, making it suitable for stereo use.

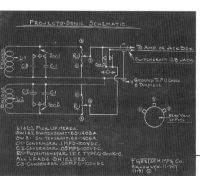

Project-O-Sonic plan (left) Gretsch bestowed their stereo guitar system with the 'Project-O-Sonic' title which, like much of the company's marketing terminology, sounded impressive... but actually meant very little. The blueprint schematic shown here is dated November 1957, indicating that it was drawn up early in Gretsch's stereo guitar project.

32

White Falcon Stereo 1962
(below) This early twin-cutaway version retains the control layout of its one-cutaway predecessor. From 1965 controls were re-arranged as in the main picture.

Stereo made simple (left) Jimmie Webster drew the original chart shown here in order to explain the intricacies of the switching system of the four-plus-one-selector stereo circuit that the company introduced in 1959. On the chart Webster calculated that six tone settings and nine pickup combinations gave the player an overwhelming "54 colors and shadings in stereo sound".

Headstock (above) Despite the changes made elsewhere on the guitar, the White Falcon's distinctive 'dipped' headstock shape was retained.

Pad on the back (above) The circular pad fixed to the back of the body on certain Gretsch models was intended to increase player comfort. It also conveniently obscured the plate over the access hole that revealed the guitar's innards.

Falcon flyer c1966 (left) This mid-1960s sheet shows the White Falcon Stereo in all its gimmick-laden glory.

35

"so I saw that Gretsch had their green Country Club and the White Falcon. We offered our colors to diversify and get another product on the market." He also says that, despite earlier Gretsch and Gibson models featuring gold-plated hardware, it was the White Falcon that finally alerted Fender to the visual bonus of gold. "We couldn't be outdone," was Randall's analysis – and from around 1957 Fender began to offer some of its models with an option of gold-plated hardware.

In the same way as Gretsch had issued a companion 'solidbody' to the Chet Atkins Hollow Body, it also produced a partner to the White Falcon in its standard-shape semi-solid style. This was called the White Penguin, complete with all the Falcon features and also released around 1955. "The name came about because a penguin has a white front," insists Duke Kramer, although it's hard to imagine how Gretsch expected anyone to buy a guitar with such an unappealing and comical name. The instrument even had a little penguin waddling across the pickguard.

In fact, very few people *did* buy the White Penguin. It doesn't appear in any of the company's catalogs, and only makes a fleeting appearance on a 1959 pricelist (at a steep $490). From the small number that surface one can presume that very few Penguins were made, and the model has since become regarded as one of the most desirable of all Gretsch guitars. Thus the occasional examples that do turn up command very high prices on the collectors' market: for example, a 1957 Gretsch White Penguin was sold by a leading New York dealer in 1992 for a staggering $70,000.

STRUM AN' SING IN COLOR

When Gretsch came to compile its 1955 catalog, it decided to pull out all the stops and create a document that would show off its new models and bright finishes to best effect. Gretsch produced a striking brochure with a cover that, unusually for guitar companies at the time, was in full color (see page 2). Over the outside front and back covers were displayed eight vivid models, including Convertible and Streamliner in two-tone finishes, a green Country Club, tan

Corvette and, of course, a White Falcon. Gretsch also took the opportunity to parade in color the two Chet Atkins models on the inside front (see page 13), plus the Duo Jet, Round Up and the recently added red Jet Fire Bird on the inside back (see page 16).

"One look at these new Gretsch guitars will tell you why musicians all over the country are raving about them," wrote Jimmie Webster inside the catalog, gazing out at the reader from behind his Country Club. "Whether you play hillbilly, jazz, progressive or just plain strum an' sing, there's a Gretsch guitar for you," he continued, modestly hinting that Gretsch now had a line which catered for virtually all the guitar-playing tastes of the era.

Phil Grant worked with the company's ad agency Mitchell Morrison to produce Gretsch's catalogs, including the peach of '55, and remembers that the resulting literature wasn't necessarily representative of the company's line at the time of publication. "There was always a deadline," he recalls, "and there would be guitars you were working on that you couldn't get into the catalog because you didn't have them finished enough to photograph. That was a normal problem. The idea was to get the guitars together so that they could be in the next catalog, but of course the catalog came out and there would always be some new models that would come out after the catalog." In other words, it would be a mistake to rely solely on contemporary catalogs to date model changes.

SAL SAYS DAN'S YOUR MAN

As the number of models in the Gretsch electric guitar line increased and the profile of the company was being raised by glossy new brochures and popular endorsers, it was decided to employ a quality-control person to ensure that what was actually coming out of the factory was equal to all this fresh attention. The new man to join the guitar team at the Brooklyn factory in 1956 was 24 year-old Dan Duffy, who'd been studying guitar with New York jazzman Sal Salvador.

Salvador played a Gretsch Convertible model, introduced in 1955 and so-called because it combined electric and acoustic properties by mounting a pickup and associated controls on the pickguard, thus avoiding interference with the resonance of the archtop body. Salvador became so associated with the Convertible that toward the end of the 1950s Gretsch renamed it the Sal Salvador model.

Constantly in touch with Gretsch, Salvador knew that they wanted a young, keen player like Duffy to work as a quality controller. Duffy recalls the set-up at the factory when he started: "I was in the small assembly department where they put the pickups and tailpieces on, strung the guitars up, tuned and adjusted them. It was up on the ninth floor of the ten-story Gretsch building. Guitars were made on two of the floors at that time; the rest was let to other people. Next door to us was the machine shop where they made bridges, tailpieces and so on, and then next to that was the plating department.

"Down on the seventh floor was the wood shop and the finishing room, where they sprayed the guitars, and beyond that area at the time was the shipping department, which dealt with Fred Gretsch's wholesale business: accordions, banjos, band instruments, that type of thing. The other part of the seventh floor was taken up with the drum department. As the years went by the drums were moved out, the finishing department became immense and guitars were made throughout the whole area. But that's how it was in the 1950s and into the first part of the 1960s."

Duffy emphasizes the key role played by the foremen throughout the Gretsch factory. So often company histories concentrate on the management figures and top people, whereas the products that define an operation's success wouldn't exist without the skills of the workers on the shop floor. "Probably Fred Gretsch's success was due to surrounding himself with good players and good foremen," Duffy suggests. "When I got there some of those guys had already been there 25 years. These guys were super-mechanics, experienced tool and die makers, they were devoted to him and to that company."

He runs through a roll-call of some of the foremen who made Gretsch guitars happen: Vincent DiDomenico and Jerry Perito (wood shop); Jimmy Capozzi (plating); Sid Laiken (machine shop); Johnny DiRosa (finishing); Felix Provet (assembly); and Carmine Coppola (repairs). "We all got along so great," Duffy reminisces. "If we had problems with rejected guitars, finishes, whatever, everyone would help out everyone else. It was like one big family."

QC Job and the OK Card

When Duffy was interviewed for his quality-control job in 1956, Jimmie Webster explained to him a new system of cards they would use that would enable a running check to be kept on a guitar's progress through the factory. Each 'OK Card', as they were known, had checks for Finish, Workmanship, Construction, Nut, Bridge, Action, Intonation, Electrical Equip. and Playing Test, plus a space for a quality controller's signature at the bottom (an example is shown on the back of the jacket, another on page 42). "Throughout the years," recalls Duffy, "we had a quality control meeting once a week where each foreman would discuss any problems. There were always finishing problems: scratches, nicks, dents, dust in the finish that had to be buffed out. Then in the wood shop the hand-sanding had to be perfect: the better the wood is sanded, the better the finish lays on. There were periods where we had neck pitch problems, wood shrinkage problems, and binding problems, especially on the White Falcon guitars. But we tackled that whole thing together. There was a lot of talent in that company, and that's what made it work."

Prices for Gretsch's 11-model electric guitar line-up were detailed in the company's catalog published in the October 1956 issue of *Country & Western Jamboree*. There were six archtops: the Clipper at $175 (in sunburst; a two-tone Desert Beige/Shadow Metallic Gray option was priced at $185); the Streamliner at $250 (sunburst; two-tone Bamboo Yellow/Copper Mist was $260; natural $260); Convertible $320; Chet Atkins Hollow Body $400; Country Club $400 (sunburst; Cadillac Green $420; natural $420); and White Falcon $650. Five semi-solids completed the picture: the Duo Jet at $290; Jet Fire Bird $300; Silver Jet $310; Round Up $350; and Chet Atkins Solid Body $400.

37

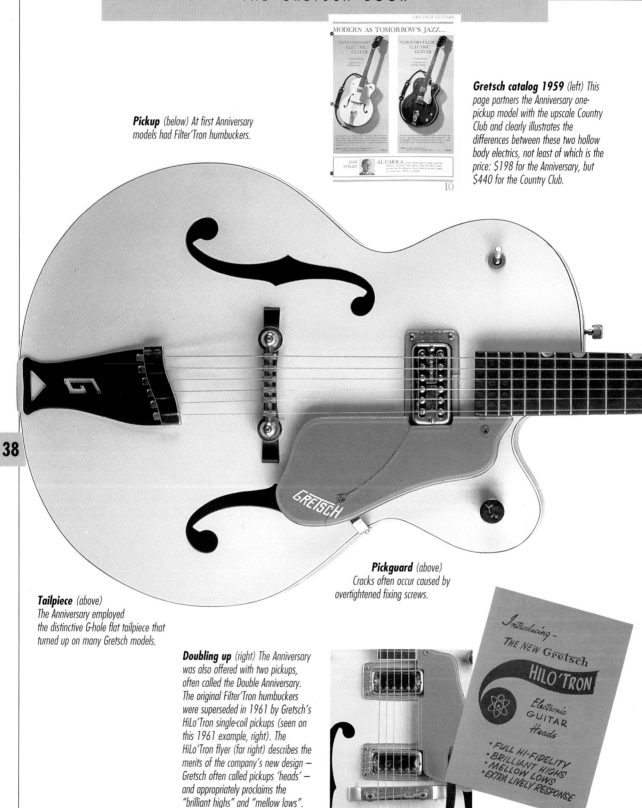

Gretsch catalog 1959 (left) This page partners the Anniversary one-pickup model with the upscale Country Club and clearly illustrates the differences between these two hollow body electrics, not least of which is the price: $198 for the Anniversary, but $440 for the Country Club.

Pickup (below) At first Anniversary models had Filter'Tron humbuckers.

Tailpiece (above)
The Anniversary employed the distinctive G-hole flat tailpiece that turned up on many Gretsch models.

Pickguard (above)
Cracks often occur caused by overtightened fixing screws.

Doubling up (right) The Anniversary was also offered with two pickups, often called the Double Anniversary. The original Filter'Tron humbuckers were superseded in 1961 by Gretsch's HiLo'Tron single-coil pickups (seen on this 1961 example, right). The HiLo'Tron flyer (far right) describes the merits of the company's new design — Gretsch often called pickups 'heads' — and appropriately proclaims the "brilliant highs" and "mellow lows".

Anniversary 1959 (below) In typically unpredictable style, Gretsch chose to commemorate their 75th anniversary (1883-1958) by issuing a budget-price model in one- and two-pickup form. The descriptively titled Anniversary models carried a suitable nameplate on the headstock to denote their special status, and about the only hint of luxury was the attractive two-tone green version shown here (back below). The model was further downgraded in the early 1960s when Gretsch substituted the unbound ebony fingerboard with cheaper rosewood and replaced Filter'Tron humbuckers with HiLo'Tron single-coils.

HAPPY ANNIVERSARY FROM GRETSCH!

Headstock (below) A diamond on the nameplate for Gretsch's 75 years.

Anniversary celebrations (above) This ad from a February 1958 music trade magazine announces the 75th anniversary of the Gretsch company and displays the products launched to commemorate the occasion. A smartly attired gent proudly shows off a two-tone one-pickup Anniversary, and the text alludes to the new guitar's relative cheapness by describing it to dealers as "priced for promotional selling".

39

Chet Atkins sleeve 1960 (above) This LP cover employs an intriguing shot which shows Chet 'at home' in the studio casually playing a one-pickup Tennessean, with other interesting Gretsches close at hand.

Chet Atkins Tennessean 1960 (above) Debuting in 1958, this was the last and cheapest of the Chet Atkins archtop trio. Until 1961 it sported a single Filter'Tron humbucker pickup located near the bridge, partnered by bare-bones circuitry comprising a volume control plus one tone selector.

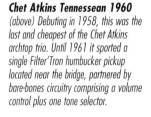

Chet Atkins Country Gentleman 1961 (right) Launched in 1957 and boasting twin Filter'Tron humbuckers, fake f-holes and Bigsby vibrato, this was top dog of the trio of Chet Atkins models. This is a late example of the first version: new twin-cutaway body styling was introduced later in 1961.

One of the musical categories that Jimmie Webster didn't mention in his round-up of guitar styles in the 1955 Gretsch catalog was rock'n'roll. Hit records through 1956 and 1957 for acts like Chuck Berry, Bill Haley & His Comets, Buddy Holly, Jerry Lee Lewis, Carl Perkins, Elvis Presley and Gene Vincent & His Blue Caps spread the popularity of this new phenomenon that would eventually sweep the old guard from the musical map and put American teenagers at the helm as the course was set for modern pop music.

$420 WORTH OF TWANG

Gretsch benefited from two big success stories in early rock'n'roll, both of whom used Chet Atkins Hollow Body guitars to power their sound. Eddie Cochran was an accomplished guitarist who started out as a session player, but in 1956 his moody good looks landed him a cameo spot in the film *The Girl Can't Help It* performing 'Twenty Flight Rock'. This led to a record deal, and Cochran subsequently made such blasting rock'n'roll singles as the classic 'Summertime Blues', with his Gretsch Hollow Body at the center of a churning mix of rockabilly, country and blues. While on first hearing Cochran seemed light years away from Chet Atkins' own musical stylings, Cochran at least seemed to agree about the quality of Gretsch's DeArmond pickups, replacing the pickup nearest the neck on his Hollow Body with a fatter-sounding Gibson P90. More hits like 'C'mon Everybody' followed, but tragically Cochran's career was cut short when he was killed in a car crash while on tour in Britain in 1960.

Duane Eddy turned out a string of hit records from the late 1950s, based on his deceptively simple instrumental style that will forever be known by the word attached to so many of his albums: Twang. That twangy tone came when Eddy concentrated on playing melodies on the bass strings of his Gretsch Hollow Body and making full use of the pitchbending potential of the guitar's Bigsby vibrato, his amplifier's tremolo, and the studio's echo facilities, resulting in gloriously haunting hits such as 'Rebel Rouser'.

Eddy recalls that his first decent electric guitar, at age 15,

was a Gibson Les Paul gold-top. Growing up in Phoenix, Arizona, and playing in high-school bands, Eddy used to check out the local music store, Ziggie's Accordion & Guitar Studios. One day in 1957 the 19 year-old Eddy made what turned out to be a very important visit. "I just went into the store with a friend of mine to look around. My Les Paul didn't have a vibrato on it, and I wanted that bar: Chet Atkins had it and Merle Travis had it. I could play the fingerpicking thing a little, but I wanted to do the vibrato part.

"So I went in the store and looked around, and there was a White Falcon hanging on the wall, which was beautiful but it was a lot of money, nearly $700. I said, 'What have you got that's nice but not so expensive?' Ziggie pulled out two or three guitars, and the first one I opened was the [$420] Hollow Body. It was the first time I saw the red Gretsch, with a Bigsby on it, and I settled on that. Took one last look at the White Falcon, but the neck wasn't as nice on it as the red Gretsch, and I didn't care for the gold trim which looked a little chintzy.

"But the red Gretsch, first time I picked it up it just took to me, settled right in there, the neck was just perfect. There's nothing more exciting than finding a new guitar, but that was such an experience that I've not bought many new ones since then. Felt no need for it." Eddy found that the Hollow Body's DeArmond pickups suited his style well. "I think Duane Eddy was the only one who liked the DeArmond pickups," laughs Chet Atkins. "He got a big bass sound out of those things."

FILTER OUT HUM, ELECTRONICALLY

Other than some flirtations with Danelectro six-string basses beginning in the late 1950s and a Guild 'signature' guitar for live work in the early 1960s, Duane Eddy has been served well by that original Chet Atkins Hollow Body (pictured on pages 20/21), right through his long and successful career. As he plans his latest album in the mid 1990s, Eddy pauses to reflect on that golden time in the late 1950s and early 1960s: "I probably sold more Gretsch guitars than anybody other than Chet Atkins," he chuckles.

When Chet Atkins met Ray Butts, a music store owner and electronics wiz from Cairo, Illinois, the guitarist's difficulties with Gretsch DeArmond pickups were about to come to an end.

Butts had gone to Nashville in 1954 to seek out the guitarists based there and attempt to interest them in his combination amplifier which offered echo from a built-in tape loop, an unusual facility at the time. Players were becoming used to echo effects in the studio, and Butts reckoned that many would jump at the opportunity to make similar sounds on stage. Chet Atkins – along with players like Elvis Presley's guitarist Scotty Moore – became a customer for Butts' new EchoSonic amp, and the two got talking about other topics of common interest. Butts helped Atkins choose recording equipment for his garage studio, and then the subject turned naturally to Atkins' quest for an improved design of guitar pickup.

"He didn't like the DeArmond pickups Gretsch were using at the time," Butts recalls. "It just didn't fit his style of playing then, he said they didn't sound right. Primarily what he wanted was a proper balance between the bass and the treble and mid-range, for that thumb effect he used, and he really didn't get it with those pickups. For one thing the magnets were too strong: they kept 'sucking' the strings and stopping the sustain. I saw some where he'd broken the bass-string magnets in two in a vise with a hammer.

"So he said to me, 'Why don't you make me a pickup?' I had done some experimenting with pickups before, so I said OK. My idea from the beginning was to build a humbucking pickup. I knew about the concept from working with transformers, and Ampex used the humbucking principle in the pickups of their recording heads. It wasn't a new idea, and it's a very simple principle," explains Butts.

The main intention of a humbucker pickup is to reduce the hum and electrical interference that afflicts standard single-coil pickups, and the ability of such devices to 'buck' (or cut) hum provides their name. A humbucking pickup employs two coils wired together out of phase and with opposite magnetic polarities. The result is a pickup that is less prone to picking up extraneous noise, and incidentally gives a more powerful and 'thicker' tone that some players prefer compared to the thinner, more trebly sound of a single-coil type.

Butts made a prototype and took it to Atkins, who was immediately impressed. "He showed me that pickup and I got in touch with Gretsch," says Atkins. "I told them this guy has an improved pickup that I like, and it gets the sound I want." As it turned out, the timing was dead right, as a change of pickup was going to suit Gretsch as well. Duke Kramer: "We wanted to drop DeArmond, because all of a sudden they were building pickups for anybody and everybody. It had become no great asset to have a DeArmond pickup on a Gretsch guitar, because other makers were putting them on cheap guitars as well as on expensive guitars. So we were very anxious to make this deal when it came up because we needed another pickup."

Butts went to New York to meet with Fred Gretsch Jr. and Jimmie Webster at the company offices in Brooklyn, probably during 1956. "They wanted to make the pickup themselves because they wanted to be sure of having supply. I wasn't experienced at manufacturing," explains Butts, "so I agreed to that. We came to an agreement on a royalty basis, I furnished all the information and everything to make the pickups, and they went and got tooling. I worked real closely with Jimmie, and I designed new control assemblies and switching to go with the new pickups."

It seems likely that the first showing of the new Gretsch-made pickup was at the summer 1957 NAMM show in Chicago. Gretsch was not alone in displaying a humbucking pickup: Gibson too had developed such a unit and it also probably showed a humbucker off to the trade for the first time that summer in Chicago. Seth Lover, who had worked permanently for Gibson's electronics department since 1952, had been inspired in his application of the humbucking principle by some Gibson amplifiers which had a 'choke coil' installed to eliminate the hum produced by the power transformer.

It appears that Butts and Lover came up with their ideas for a humbucking pickup independently and at around the same time – although Lover did manage to file his patent much earlier than Butts. "I feel I was first with it," Butts insists. "It's

Ronny Lee in B.M.G (above)
American guitarist and teacher Ronny
Lee is featured with his signature
Gretsch model on the cover of the
March 1968 issue of this UK music
magazine (B.M.G. meant
Banjo, Mandolin,
Guitar).

OK Card (right) Each Gretsch guitar
came with a card like this confirming
that it had been passed by the
company's quality control department.

F-holes (below) These 'fake'
f-holes are painted onto the
guitar's body.

Chet Atkins Hollow Body 1961

(left) In 1961 twin-cutaway styling was introduced for certain models, and on this guitar was accompanied by fake f-holes, plus a string damper and control. This early example is in red rather than the more usual orange.

Gretsch catalog 1963 (left)

Gretsch presented the Chet Atkins series proudly in the 1963 catalog, with this colorful line-up – brown Country Gent, red Tennessean, orange Hollow Body – putting in an impressive appearance. The Tennessean was the only one of the Chet Atkins models which did not switch with its companions to the new twin-cutaway design in the early 1960s.

Chet Atkins Teen Scene (left)

Keeping in with the in crowd, Chet is seen on this album cover shot with the new twin-cutaway Hollow Body, another trendy sweater, an apparently hard-working drummer, a packed dance floor and the requisite gaggle of adoring young fans. Heaven.

43

Chet Atkins Hollow Body 1962

(above) Finished in the more familiar orange, this example has all the relevant aspects of the period such as zero fret, twin-cutaway styling, fake f-holes, string damper and (not shown) padded back. Nonetheless it continues to employ a single-saddle bridge.

Inlays (above) Note the double half-moon markers (see also page 58/59).

Ronny Lee 1962 (above)

This limited-production guitar was made for Ronny Lee, a New York-based player, teacher and retailer. It incorporates features from other Gretsch models, such as large fake f-holes and twin HiLo'Tron single-coil pickups. Although some examples came in sunburst, this example is in a deep brown, displaying the nicely flamed wood to good effect, particularly on the back (right).

conception that counts, and I feel I had better documentation on that: I had pictures of Chet playing a guitar with my pickups on it in 1954, for example. But Gibson complained, and Mr. Gretsch discussed it with Mr. McCarty at Gibson. They decided to let each go his own way without the other one challenging."

In typically grand style Gretsch called its new humbucker pickup the Filter'Tron Electronic Guitar Head. The bombast continued in the company's explanatory leaflet: "Good electronic reproducing units such as Hi-Fidelity, Stereophonic and such, have created a demand for perfect sound and performance... It is with this knowledge in mind that we present the new Filter'Tron heads for guitar. The finest engineers in the country were engaged in the development of the Filter'Tron and their main object was to produce the greatest sound with as many color combinations as possible." This patter has always amused Ray Butts. "'The finest engineers in the country.' That was me!" he laughs. "But they never associated me with anything, in the literature, advertising, anything else. Of course, they had their interest. But there's people to this day don't know I had anything to do with those pickups."

By 1958 Gretsch was advertising Filter'Trons as standard on all models except the thinline Clipper (for which Gretsch came up with its own single-coil pickup, the HiLo'Tron). There was also a new control layout devised by Ray Butts to complement the Filter'Trons. A two-pickup guitar would have a volume control for each pickup in the normal position at the bottom of the body, plus a master volume on the cutaway bout. On the top bout there were two three-way switches: the one furthest from the player was a normal both-or-either pickup selector, and the other switch was for "tone color", selecting between neutral, bass-emphasis or treble-emphasis settings.

DARK BROWN GENT, LOWLY TENNESSEAN

Two new models in the Chet Atkins series were released in 1957 and 1958, the Country Gentleman and the Tennessean. "I had a hit record in the mid 1950s called 'Country Gentleman' which I wrote with Boudleaux Bryant," Atkins says. Bryant was a very successful songwriter, probably best known for penning a number of Everly Brothers hits. "When 'Country Gentleman' had been a hit I guess it was probably Gretsch's idea to put out another model," Atkins continues. "They were selling so many of the orange Gretsch they wanted to put out a little more expensive guitar. So the Country Gentleman had good tuning pegs, better wood selection, and the body was generally a little larger and thinner. I started to use the Country Gentleman on my records continually. I would use the Hollow Body once in a while – I know I've seen pictures of me with it in the studio – but I didn't use it as much as I used the Country Gentleman."

The Country Gent was the first Gretsch archtop to be made with a 'thinline' body – about two inches deep, unlike most of its existing archtops which were around three inches deep. The Thinline concept had been popularized by Gibson in the preceding years with its Byrdland and ES-350T models. Also worth noting is the fact that the Country Gentleman was the first Gretsch Chet Atkins model to be offered with a slightly wider 17-inch body, like the White Falcon, Country Club and Convertible. The Hollow Body (and indeed the new Tennessean) was closer to 16 inches wide.

"Guitar star Chet Atkins will be in the Gretsch Guitar room to greet you personally," the company informed its dealers in preparation for the summer 1957 NAMM show in Chicago. The dark brown Gent was previewed there, and its price of $525 put it second only to the White Falcon in the company's archtop electric line.

WHEN IS AN F-HOLE NOT AN F-HOLE?

Chet Atkins had for some time been pressing Gretsch to address some of the problems experienced with hollow-body electrics. As live music, especially rock'n'roll, began to be performed at louder volumes on stage, guitarists playing hollow-body electrics often found themselves plagued by howling feedback when they turned their amplifiers up too high. Feedback is caused by guitar pickups picking up their own sound from the amplifier's loudspeakers, and then feeding it back into the system, creating an unpleasant 'howlround' effect. The increasingly amplified soundwaves move into and around the guitar's body, agitating the top and setting up vibrations which in turn promote more feedback.

Atkins and Gretsch decided that one way to diminish this unwanted effect was to block off the f-holes in the guitar's body, and the Country Gentleman appeared in 1957 with what are generally referred to as 'fake' f-holes. In other words, there is a visual representation of the f-holes on the body, to help the general look of the guitar, but there are no actual apertures. At first the f-holes were blocked with plastic or wooden infills; later, and when 'fake' f-holes were applied to other Gretsch models (of which more later), they were simply painted on. Atkins recalls that an early sample, sent to him by Gretsch to check if the idea of closed f-holes was workable, had the filled f-holes covered with sparkle material (see the guitar pictured on page 32).

Atkins tried to convince Gretsch that in order to cut feedback – and moreover to enhance his beloved sustain – it would also be useful to make the instrument's hollow body more solid at certain points by adding wooden reinforcement inside. In fact, what Atkins wanted was a guitar that had a solid wooden section running through the center of the body from neck to tailpiece – exactly as Gibson did on its ES-335 model that debuted in 1958. This solid center was also needed to mount the bridge and humbucking pickups that Gibson used at the time, but as Gretsch employed a floating bridge and non-height-adjustable humbuckers it had no need for this facility. Gretsch was content merely to add twin strengthening braces under the top of the Country Gentleman's body.

Atkins, however, was less than content. "I continually tried to get them to make the guitar more solid from the neck down to the end," he remembers. "I wanted more of a sturdy guitar that was more sustained. Originally the Country Gent did have two braces that went from the end of the guitar to the neck, but they didn't join it, so it still killed off the sustain. They finally made it semi-solid back to the bridge, and had a piece of wood going out to the back, which helped, but it didn't go all the way to the end of the guitar. They never could do that for me."

The other new Chet Atkins model was the red Tennessean issued in 1958 at $295, about $100 less than the Hollow Body. Gretsch now had three Chet Atkins models in its line priced at low ($295 Tennessean), middle ($400 Hollow Body) and upper-mid ($525 Country Gentleman) levels. Naturally Gretsch hoped this would secure them a bigger share of the market that Gibson was still dominating. Around this time, in an ad aimed at music store owners, Fred Gretsch Jr. underlined the importance of having products spanning all price-points: "You can capitalize on the range of taste and spending much more easily than the auto industry. Gretsch can supply you and your customers with 'Cadillac' or 'Volkswagen' models. Write me personally for details..."

MELITA TO SPACE CONTROL, OVER...

A number of new features began to appear around this time, including in 1957 control knobs with Gretsch's classic 'arrow-through-G' design on the top, but more noticeable was the latest bridge, the Space Control. No doubt the company reasoned that if it could now make pickups in-house, then it could certainly make its own bridges – enabling it to dispense with Mr. Melita's services as well as Mr. DeArmond's and thereby gain more control over the production and supply of key components.

The Space Control bridge was a Jimmie Webster design, and was a lot simpler than Melita's Synchro-Sonic unit. It had six wheel-like grooved saddles each of which could be positioned as desired along a threaded bar, but intonation adjustment was not possible. Gretsch obviously considered the benefits outweighed such drawbacks, and began to replace the Melita bridge with the Space Control from 1957.

Also new was the Neo-Classic fingerboard, which once again Gretsch eulogized in a handy leaflet: "Centuries ago, when string instruments were first built, the early craftsmen discovered that pure ebony offered the best playing performance, and that discovery stands to this very day. As time passed, man decided to decorate these fine playing boards with fancy pearl inlays which were beautiful but in no way helped

CORVETTE

- NEW CURVED SHAPE WITH CARVED EDGES
- SOLID MAHOGANY IN CHERRY RED FINISH

PX6134

Corvette with its dashing double cutaway design brings the colossal gamut of the full Gretsch tone and chromatic ease of playing. This full toned compact instrument is bound to be the envy of musicians everywhere.

Designed for speed and fingering ease in the high register with neck joined to body at 21st fret. Solid Mahogany neck and body with 24½" scale. Body finished in brilliant Cherry Red. Rosewood fingerboard. Adjustable truss rod neck. Gretsch HiLo'Tron electric pick-up. On model PX6134(T) the exclusive Gretsch V-brato for that exciting tremolo effect. Leather shoulder strap. Chrome plated metal parts. Body size only 13½" x 1½" x 19" long.

PX6132 Gretsch Corvette Guitar in Cherry Red, single pickup (not illustrated) .... 70 gns.

PX6134 Gretsch Corvette Guitar in Cherry Red with exclusive Gretsch V-brato, single pickup .... 87 gns.

PX6135 Gretsch Corvette Guitar in Cherry Red with exclusive Gretsch V-brato and Double Pickup (not illustrated) .... 110 gns.

Gretsch catalog 1963 (above) This shows the amended Corvette design, the basic solidbody now coming with one or two HiLo'Trons and an optional vibrato tailpiece. The new body shape lost the 'slab' look and gained some style, but its beveled-edge outline again followed Gibson's lead, this time recalling their SG Junior.

46

Corvette c1961 (left) Gretsch introduced this model, their first true solidbody guitar, in 1961. Using a name from a 1950s non-cutaway hollow body, this basic model borrowed heavily from Gibson's double-cutaway Les Paul Junior in construction, wood, 'slab' body styling and pickup layout (in this case a bridge-position HiLo'Tron). Also offered in gray, this example is the alternative brown version. (The control knobs are later replacements.)

Twist c1963 (right) Designed to cash in on the big dance craze of the period was this colorful variant of the revised Corvette. The latter now had a more streamlined, beveled-edge body which mimicked Gibson's restyled SG Junior. The Twist came in bright red (or the more unusual yellow shown) with a striking red and white striped pickguard. Here a 'Space Control' bridge replaces the single-saddle type used on this cheaper model.

GRETSCH GUITARS

Give you the Arbiter Sound

ELECTRIC | Hollow-Solid | FLAT TOP · FOLK · CLASSIC

Gretsch UK catalog 1963 (above) Here the British importer of Gretsch guitars, J.I. Arbiter Ltd., opted for some self-publicity that resulted in the amusingly confusing title, "Gretsch Guitars give you the Arbiter sound".

'Gold Jet' 1962 (right) Although different color sparkle body fronts were offered from about 1962, these were actually listed in Gretsch literature until about 1963 as options of the Silver Jet. So the 'Gold Jet' shown is officially a Silver Jet in gold sparkle — surely another instance of Gretsch's habitually illogical approach. As with all the Jet variants, this model received the revised twin-cutaway body shape in 1961. The only other major change was the more frequent use of a vibrato tailpiece, in this case designed and made by British guitar company, Burns. The move from the US Bigsby type may have been due to Bigsby's supply problems, which also affected Gibson and Rickenbacker around the same time.

Gretsch catalog 1961 (above) This pictures the revised semi-solid Jet series which all now feature Gretsch's new twin-cutaway body styling.

'Silver Jet' 1969 (right) From about 1963 different sparkle body-front colors were officially Duo Jet options — in which case this example was (as far as the company was concerned) a Duo Jet with a silver sparkle front. The gold plastic and hardware makes an unusual and impressive contrast, and by this late date the Burns vibrato was long gone, with Bigsby back in favor.

the playing performance of the board; it only destroyed the wonderful feel only pure satin ebony could give.

"It is with these proven facts in mind that we introduce the new Gretsch Neo Classic fingerboard – the finest in playing performance and sheer beauty. The beautifully inlaid mother-of-pearl half moons on the bass side of the board are perfect position markers and do not in any way detract from the classic feel which is so essential to perfect performance. Neo Classic construction preserves the full strength of the fingerboard." How could you refuse? The Neo-Classic half moons rose along Gretsch fingerboards during 1958.

That same year Gretsch decided to mark the 75th anniversary of the company's founding and, having already tried the idea with 70th anniversary accordions in 1953, issued special Anniversary model guitars in one- and two-pickup versions. They were launched with all the new appointments – Filter'Tron pickups, arrow-through-G knobs, Space Control bridges and Neo-Classic fingerboards – and were offered in an attractive two-tone green as well as sunburst. Remarkably enough for instruments related to the importance of a solitary year in the company's history, they lasted in the line until 1977. While the relatively downscale Anniversary guitars constituted something of a cheap celebration – "priced for promotional selling" was the euphemism employed by Gretsch's ad copywriter – at least the party was a long one.

TWO GUITARS FOR THE PRICE OF ONE

'Stereo' and 'stereophonic' were magic words in the late 1950s, heralding all that was new and exciting in sound reproduction. During 1956 RCA Victor released the first commercial stereo pre-recorded tapes, and later the first stereo LPs were issued by the major American record labels. Immersed in the potential of electronics and sound, Jimmie Webster put his fertile brain to work on the possibilities of a stereo guitar.

Part of Ray Butts' deal with Gretsch over their use of the Filter'Tron pickups involved his availability as a consultant. He remembers the call. "Jimmie asked me to design a stereo pickup. It was basically quite simple: just take the Filter'Tron

and split the windings. Normally you have one winding that covers all six strings. If you cut it in half, you have two separate sets of windings, making three strings independent of the other three. You bring the signals from these windings out separately to separate controls and send them to separate amplifiers. So when you pick the first three strings it comes out of this amp, and the top three strings come out of that amp."

That in a nutshell is Gretsch's stereo Project-O-Sonic system, the subject of a Jimmie Webster patent filed in December 1956. A normal Filter'Tron had two parallel rows of six polepieces visible, but the splitting of the pickups for the first Project-O-Sonic set-up usually resulted in only half the number of polepieces being evident: on the left side of the front pickup, under the three bass strings, and on the right side of the bridge pickup, beneath the three treble strings. However, the experimental nature of these instruments means that varieties exist, and examples with one row of six poles plus a half-row of three have been seen, as well as normal-looking 12-pole units with the splitting accomplished internally. The bridge pickup is also located much closer to the neck pickup than usual.

The control layout and functions were similar to a normal guitar with two Filter'Trons, but the master volume knob on the cutaway bout was replaced with a three-way switch that selected various combinations of pickups and amps, while the two switches on the upper bout offered independent control of tonal emphasis for each pickup. A special Dual Guitar Cord connected the guitar to a Dual Jack Box, which provided two more jacks to connect to the two amplifiers necessary for stereo reproduction (Gretsch offered their own pair to make a complete stereo outfit).

The Project-O-Sonic stereo system was launched as an option available on the Country Club and White Falcon models during 1958, and an ad in February noted "magnificent new electronic guitars" with "revolutionary built-in hi-fi sound systems", while a September news item described "stereophonic bi-aural sound". The Country Club Stereo was priced at $475 in sunburst and $20 more for natural or green finishes, while the White Falcon Stereo was $850, which at $175 more than a normal Falcon placed it clearly at the top of the Gretsch tree.

Jimmie Webster recorded an album for RCA in December 1958, *Unabridged*, where he made full use of his White Falcon Stereo. No doubt Gretsch was delighted: from its point of view the 1959 album amounted to a high-profile demo of its new stereo guitar. Indeed the stereo version of the album must be among the first stereo records released to feature electric guitar. The LP was produced by Chet Atkins, and was originally recorded at a studio in Nashville. Phil Grant: "Jimmie made the album with a drummer down there under Chet's tutelage, but I believe there was some kind of technical fault with the recording, and he had to do it over again in New York. They had to have another drummer there, so they got me. My percussion thing was really just to tone up what Jimmie was doing, so that there was something there besides guitar. We had rehearsed quite a bit, so the session went without any hitches."

For a change, Gibson had to follow Gretsch's lead, and issued their own interpretation of the stereo guitar idea in 1959, first with the ES-345 and then the ES-355. However, Gibson's more straightforward system directed the output of each complete pickup to separate amps. Gretsch for its part soon modified its first stereo guitar process, and a more complex version began to appear in 1959.

Webster had proposed an alternative stereo set-up to Butts back in summer 1957, but it was almost a year before Gretsch managed to get a test-bed instrument to Butts so that he could find out how the ideas would work on an actual guitar (see page 32). By early 1959 the new Gretsch stereo circuitry was ready, and factory manager Harold Woods wrote to Butts to tell him that they expected to show the first sample of the White Falcon with the new stereo system at the company's Guitarama show in Boston in April.

Visitors to the Boston demo would have seen a White Falcon with conventional looking Filter'Trons but a more complex control layout. Webster and Butts had once again split the 12 poles of each pickup into two, this time always internally with no visible evidence, while adding two more three-way switches on the upper bout to give the guitar a total of three control knobs and five selectors. The new pair provided nine combinations of the split pickup sections, and Gretsch calculated that the six tonal options provided by the other two selectors gave a grand total of "54 colors and shadings in stereo sound". Presumably the Boston audience would have needed a bit of time to think that one over.

The new system was built into a White Falcon Stereo that was pictured together with a 'mono' example on the cover of Gretsch's 1959 catalog (although surprisingly neither was featured in detail within). The second-type Falcon Stereo was made available for sale during 1959, while the revised version of the Country Club Stereo appeared in the following year. Gretsch also issued an Anniversary Stereo in 1961 which went back to the original control layout but used two split HiLo'Tron single-coil pickups.

CAR SALESMAN SHOWS OFF STEREO

These products of Webster's rich imagination and Butts' efficient technical prowess enjoyed limited sales success. Duke Kramer: "They were too complicated. A few players could use the system, but on the Falcon Stereo there was something like 54 different tone variations, and that got to be a little much for anybody to handle... and in fact there wasn't that much difference between some of the colorings. It never really became too popular."

Not that the stereo system wasn't impressive, especially in the hands of its creator. A young Philadelphia-based guitarist, Ross Finley, went to a Gretsch Guitarama promotional show at the time. Thirty years and more later, Finley still has a vivid memory of the event. "Back then the White Falcon was a legend," he says. "I'd seen a couple on television but had never seen one up close. So I found out that Jimmie Webster was coming to town with Chet Atkins, on the same bill. Come the day, a few friends and I walk in, and I see this guy standing there in the hallway, he's got a dark blue suit on, and he's beckoning to me – I guess we looked like guitar players. So we

George Harrison's Duo Jet 1957 (below) Harrison acquired this in about 1960 from a personal ad and used it to good effect in The Beatles' early years, before loaning it to a friend. He regained the Gretsch some 20 years later, and this long 'retirement' has left it in surprisingly good condition given its age and history. George and Jet are seen in a 1963 ad for amp company Vox, alongside Paul's Hofner and John's Rickenbacker.

50

Vibrato
(above) The V-cutout Bigsby appeared around 1959, suggesting a slightly later addition to this '57 Jet.

Chet Atkins (right) This 1962 ad promotes the continuing involvement of Atkins with the design of his namesake guitars. By the time this ad appeared the various 'new' features had been around for some time, and the text also erroneously allocates Filter'Tron pickups to the Tennessean. All in all it's a classic case of marketing misinformation.

Chet Atkins Nashville 1967
(below) This was a Chet Atkins Hollow
Body, retitled from 1967 and with only
the model name on the headstock and
pickguard to define the difference.

**Chet Atkins
Country Gentleman
1973** (above) By now
the Gent had real f-holes and a new
pickguard, contrasting the 1965
catalog example (right).

Position markers (below) Hump-top
blocks came in on the Jet about 1957.

51

Duo Jet rear view (right) Not too
surprisingly, the back of George
Harrison's 1957 Duo Jet shows signs of
playing wear, evidenced by the various
marks visible on the clear-finished
brown mahogany.

**Chet Atkins Country Gentleman
1963** (below) This is a 'classic' version
from this period, considered today to be
the most desirable because of the

connection with George Harrison, who
used one during The Beatles' heyday.
This fact alone guarantees its continuing
appeal to collectors.

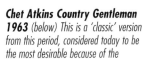

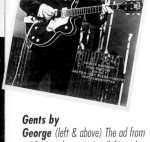

**Gents by
George** (left & above) The ad from
a 1964 trade magazine (left) and
the promo shot of Harrison reveal
Gretsch's exploitation of The Beatles.

walked up, he says, 'You fellas looking for the guitar show?' Yes. He says, 'I'm Jimmie Webster, nice to meet you.' How about that?

"So we walked into the room, there's the Gretsch catalog in living color, every Gretsch you ever saw. The stage was set up: a drum set, two Gretsch amps, and the White Falcon is sitting in the middle. Jimmie Webster came out, pulls this White Falcon up, and they shone a light show on the guitar: as he held it up and the lights hit it, it was like a rainbow. Impressive is a poor word. It's something I'll always remember.

"There was something about Jimmie Webster. He looked like a banker, or a car salesman, anything but this great guitar player. He went almost into a trance before he played, closed his eyes, concentrated for a few seconds, and then produced this incredible sound. I didn't have a very good record player at the time, everything out of one speaker, and it had never dawned on me that you could take a switch and hit a note and have this sound ping-pong between two speakers. It would start out to his left, over to the right, and back to the left. What a gimmick! Talk about impressed! Years before a wah pedal, and here's this guy doing a trick show."

Gretsch's December 1959 pricelist showed a contemporary lineup of no less than 15 electric models. There were 11 archtops: the Clipper at $175; the Anniversary one-pickup at $225; Anniversary two-pickup at $310; Chet Atkins Tennessean $325; Sal Salvador $375; Country Club $450 (sunburst; natural or Cadillac Green $475); Chet Atkins Hollow Body $475; Country Club Stereo $500 (sunburst; natural or Cadillac Green $525); Chet Atkins Country Gentleman $575; White Falcon $750; and White Falcon Stereo $900. There were four semi-solids: the Duo Jet at $310; Jet Fire Bird at $325; Silver Jet $330; and Chet Atkins Solid Body $475.

The bodies of Gretsch guitars began to change shape during the early 1960s, and the metamorphosis began when some archtops were made thinner from around 1960. Gretsch had discovered with the thinline Country Gentleman that many players preferred the more manageable feel of a slimmer guitar, and so Gretsch whittled the Falcon down from about three to two inches deep and also took a good inch off the $2^3/_4$-inch deep Country Club, as well as trimming down the Hollow Body and the Tennessean.

More spectacular was the modification of the Country Gent, Hollow Body and White Falcon to a twin-cutaway style in 1961 and 1962. Gibson was as ever the primary inspiration for this decision: since 1958 the Kalamazoo guitar-maker had increasingly employed double cutaways to successful effect. With such a body design, players could more easily reach the higher frets of the fingerboard and make fuller use of this upper register when soloing.

The new archtop twin-cutaway body applied to the Chet Atkins models was, of course, given a name: Electrotone. Following the experiment with the Country Gentleman's closed f-holes, the hollow, sealed Electrotone body generally had 'fake' f-holes stencil-painted on to maintain a reasonably traditional look for the Atkins models.

INSPECTOR GADGET

During the early 1960s Jimmie Webster continued to come up with ideas for add-on gadgetry which he felt could give Gretsch's guitars the edge over the competition. A subsequent outcrop of weird devices began to make the instruments look ever more complex as the decade progressed.

Many players regularly use the edge of their picking hand to damp strings near the bridge. To save them the trouble, Webster came up with a mechanical damper, or mute (Gretsch called it a muffler). Webster's patent for the muffler was filed in February 1962, although it had begun to appear on guitars from around 1960. Depending on the model and period, a single or double pad resides close to the bridge and under the strings. The pad(s) can be brought into contact with the strings by turning one or two 'dial-up' control knobs (later lever-action switches) situated either side of the bridge. "Eliminates need of the wrist for muffling," said a doubtful Gretsch brochure, "[and] allows complete hand freedom for playing ease." But automation was not welcome here. Most mufflers remained unraised, unused... and wrists were kept busy.

A 'standby' switch was added to the control layout of some models from 1961, and it simply turned the guitar's output on or off. The idea was that the instrument could be switched off when not being used but while still plugged in to the amplifier. The intention was *not* that it could be operated accidentally, so the standby switch was put down by the tailpiece where, it was hoped, it would be out of arm's and harm's way.

Around this time some archtop models began to receive another piece of Webster wildness, the padded back (see page 3; Webster's patent was filed June 1963). "For added comfort and playing," ran the catalog hype, "a springy pad of foam rubber on the guitar back cushions pressure and eliminates fatigue." It omitted to mention that it also conveniently hides the big, ugly control-access plate on the back of the body. Webster's daughter Jennifer remembers going with her father to obtain the padded material from a Long Island supplier of convertible tops and seating covers for cars. And Duke Kramer recalls a sort of extended version of the padded back that (thankfully) never made production: "I went to the factory one time and they showed me this padded guitar. The whole guitar was padded! Top, sides, everything. It was a real monster," he laughs. "I think Jimmie was a little upset when we laughed at him. That one didn't get across."

The Tone Twister was a Webster idea too (his patent was filed in June 1962). It was a small device that clipped onto the 'dead' string area between the bridge and tailpiece; manipulating the small arm attached would enable the brave player to induce vibrato effects. It also had the undesirable ability to achieve startling string-breaking effects, which rather limited its popularity.

GRETSCH GIZMOS, GUITAR GADGETRY

T-Zone Tempered Treble was the grand name given to Jimmie's slanted frets idea (he was down at the patent office again in February 1962 for this one). Quality control man Dan Duffy recalls: "Jimmie would tell us that when you tune a piano — remember he was a piano player and had his own piano tuning business — you always tune the upper register a little sharper than the bass, that's the way the human ear hears." And so for the Tempered Treble, Gretsch would slant the frets by one degree from the 12th fret and above, sharpening the treble strings slightly. The White Falcon and Viking models which bore this questionable addition from 1964 were marked with offset dot markers in the slanted zone. "You will never notice the slight degree in your fingering but you will notice a beautiful change in your treble range," insisted Gretsch.

Next came the Floating Sound Unit, in 1966 (patent filed August 1965), another idea that Webster pulled from his piano-tuning work. A triple-bar frame sits between bridge and muffler, the strings threaded through it. Fixed to the underside of the frame is a tuning fork that passes downwards through a hole in the top of the body, and the fork is designed to make contact with the guitar's back. The theory was that this would improve sustain, but mostly the unit would rattle around and also ruin any attempts to intonate the guitar accurately.

Many Floating Sound Units have subsequently been removed by exasperated guitarists. Webster himself tended to use a variety that left the low E-string free, which he would replace with a bass E (an octave below the guitar type), and in a Gretsch leaflet this is called the 'Octo-Bass' scheme. Chet Atkins: "Jimmie's tuning fork idea was supposed to make the guitar sustain, but the bass strings didn't have any balls. I had them make me a tuning fork that just was on the first four strings, but I never did utilize it."

Atkins goes on to explain the reasoning behind Webster's 1960s gizmos. "Jimmie said to me, 'You've got to give them something different all the time, it's like a car, you've got to come up with something new, they want new features.' And I guess he was right, he was a hell of a salesman. But I never liked them all," Atkins laughs.

And the Gretsch view? Duke Kramer: "Some of Jimmie's ideas were good, some were bad. The padded back was OK, the Tempered Treble was a little far fetched, and the Floating Sound Unit was an absolute pain in the neck." Dan Duffy: "I didn't always agree with Jimmie, but you had to train yourself to be commercially minded. You couldn't go in there every day

53

'Gold Duke' Corvette 1966
(left) This title is actually a nickname allotted by Gretsch collectors. Although suggesting a connection with Gretsch stalwart Duke Kramer, the man himself disavows any such association. In reality the 'Gold Duke' is a Corvette two-pickup solidbody finished in gold metallic, front and back (right). This was a very limited custom color; the model normally came in a red sunburst.

'Silver Duke' Corvette 1966
(left) Another nickname in common use, but Kramer's disclaimer (see text left) also applies here. However, this is an equally rare Corvette variant with a silver metallic custom-color coat to front and back (below). In 1964 the Corvette had been restyled again, acquiring a novel headstock with two tuners one side and four the other, while the body gained a small cut-out in the base to house the lower strap button. This version provided the basis for the 'Duke' duo, made for California dealer Sherman Clay, which came with standard Corvette components.

Bikini 1961 (left) This very un-Gretsch-like novelty was the brainchild of one Charles Savona, a US musician who convinced Gretsch to manufacture and market it. The Bikini was launched in 1961, and the Gretsch catalog of that year took a whole page to extol its many virtues (far left). The guitar- and bass-neck sections could be slid into body 'backs' designed to take single or double necks and hinged to facilitate compact travel. The concept was based on easy transportation and flexible operation, but the instruments were basic and plain, and predictably died an early death. Steve Howe's double-neck shown here has an added Gibson P90 pickup on the guitar side.

Astro-Jet 1966 (left & below) Introduced in 1963, this unusual looking model certainly owed nothing to Gretsch's previous solidbody models, which were quite conventional by comparison. Identity is affirmed by the metal nameplate fixed to an oddly-proportioned body that has significant beveling and a red/black two-tone color scheme (see side view below). A randomly styled headstock (four tuners one side, two the other) tops the surprisingly normal neck. Hardware includes Super'Tron humbuckers with laminated 'bar' polepieces, and a Burns-design vibrato tailpiece.

55

Roc Jet 1972 (left) The renewed success of Gibson's Les Paul guitars in the late 1960s prompted Gretsch to revive the single-cutaway styling of their early semi-solids. The Roc Jet debuted in 1969 and, despite Gretsch stylistic touches, was yet another overt follower of Gibson fashion. Even the control layout apes standard Les Paul practice, although Gretsch add a master volume on the cutaway to govern the two Super'Tron humbuckers.

and be a jazz guitar player, you had to go in there and be a businessman. Those guitars had to play right, and get the hell out the door so the money came in. That's what it was all about," affirms Duffy.

THE PRINCESS WITH THE TWISTED BIKINI

The solidbody line also went twin-cutaway from 1961, although it appears for example that very few Chet Atkins Solid Body models in this style were made, while a twin-winged White Penguin would be an even rarer find than the single-cutaway version. Soon after Gretsch changed the solids to the double-cutaway style, their Bigsby vibrato tailpieces were replaced with British Burns-designed units, probably because of supply irregularities from Bigsby. Quite why Gretsch should choose the product of a small maker from the UK is a mystery – although one can speculate that if Jimmie Webster and Jim Burns had met at a trade show they would surely have had a great time discussing wacky gadgetry. Whatever the reason, Gretsch carried on using the Burns vibratos on its solid lines into the mid 1960s.

During the earlier part of the decade Gretsch toyed with a number of oddball solidbody designs. The idea for the Bikini model was brought to the company by a local guitarist, Charles Savona, who had in mind a hinged, folding body-back which could accept slide-in, interchangeable guitar and bass necks. The body-backs would be in both single- and double-neck styles, and the result would be a versatile, portable guitar, Savona assured them. However, Dan Duffy remembers something of a struggle to bring the Bikini to production. "People at the factory worked diligently to design the 'butterfly' backs so that the track would work right. It was a great idea, but in my estimation it wasn't really engineered correctly."

A Bikini neck and back was cataloged at $175, bass neck and back $195, and a double back with guitar and bass necks $355. Single backs could be bought separately for $25, double backs for $35. Bill Hagner was made factory manager in 1961, and he too recalls that the Bikini caused some suffering at the workbenches. "You talk about a hard guitar to make," he

laughs. "Forget about it! Headache! To get that thing on correctly and sliding up and down... it was awful. We didn't make that many of the Bikini, thank god."

In 1961 Gretsch needed a cheaper solidbody to compete with Gibson's Les Paul Junior, and came up with the $139.50 Corvette. This was Gretsch's first true solidbody guitar, complete with HiLo'Tron single-coil pickup. It started life with a 'slab' body like the Junior, but subsequently gained beveled-edge contours, aping Gibson's new SG design.

An interesting variation of the later Corvette was the colorful Princess model of 1962. "For the first time in guitar manufacturing history an instrument has been selectively constructed only for girls," ran Gretsch's ad. "This is the unique adaptable Gretsch Princess Guitar, engineered with identical Gretsch precision to meet the needs and standards of young women all over the world." Gretsch had, in fact, simply finished the Corvette in special pastel color combinations designed to appeal to the delicate female sensibility. The boys at Gretsch offered "White body with Grape pickguard, Blue body with White pickguard, Pink body with White pickguard, or White body with Gold pickguard". The girls failed to respond to such charms, however, and shortly afterwards the Princess retired from public view.

Another opportunist variant of the 1962 Corvette was Gretsch's Twist model. Chubby Checker's 'The Twist' 45 had topped the US chart for the second time in January and set off the twist dance fad. "You follow a trend," explains Duke Kramer. "The twist dance was an absolute craze, everyone was doing the twist. What better than to bring out a Twist guitar?" This colored Corvette had a pickguard bearing a twisting red and white 'peppermint' design. Of course, the Twist did not last long.

Gretsch's pricelist of September 1962 sums up a line of 19 electrics. There were 12 archtops: the Clipper at $189; Anniversary one-pickup at $225; Anniversary two-pickup $295; Chet Atkins Tennessean (now two-pickup) $350; Sal Salvador $375; Anniversary Stereo $375; Chet Atkins Hollow Body $495; Country Club $495; Country Club Stereo $550; Chet

Atkins Country Gentleman $595; White Falcon $800; and White Falcon Stereo $1000. There were seven solids: the Corvette at $148 (or with vibrato $185); Twist at $149 (or with vibrato $189), Princess $169; Duo Jet $350; Jet Fire Bird $350; Silver Jet $350; and Chet Atkins Solid Body $425.

THE VIKING WITH THE PERIOD PARAPHERNALIA

The last of Gretsch's new early 1960s solidbodys was the $295 Astro-Jet, which appeared around 1963. "Hand-carved edges highlight its unusual body design," said the catalog. When Gretsch, no strangers themselves in the land of weird, said something was 'unusual' you just knew it had to be truly outlandish. The Astro-Jet was indeed a very strange looking guitar, almost as if it had been left out too long on a hot Brooklyn summer day and melted into several disfigured lumps. It was big, too: the body of the Astro-Jet measured 16 inches across, making it some three inches wider than most Gretsch solids.

On a more straightforward note, the Astro-Jet featured Gretsch's new Super'Tron humbucking pickup, visually characterized by the absence of polepieces; instead it has two long, bar-shaped, laminated poles on the top. Duke Kramer recalls the Astro-Jet as "an effort to bring out something that would compete with Fender but not look like Fender. It was a heavy guitar, an awkward shape. It didn't play too bad but it just didn't catch the imagination of the players. I don't know who was responsible for the design, but I suppose I can push it onto Jimmie Webster..."

In 1964 Gretsch launched the Viking, its first new archtop electric since the Chet Atkins Tennessean six years earlier. At $650 it was second only to the $850 White Falcon in price, and with all the paraphernalia of the period – mufflers, T-Zone frets, padded back, telescopic vibrato arm and all – could almost be considered as a mono Falcon for those who didn't fancy a white guitar with a winged headstock. The Cadillac Green Viking was, like the sunburst variety, pitched at $650, while a natural no-paint-at-all job would, perversely as ever, cost you an extra $25.

THE BEATLE WITH THE GRETSCH GUITARS

In Liverpool, England, in August 1960 a fledgling group called The Beatles set out to start a run of no less than 48 nights at the Indra club in Hamburg, northern Germany. Guitarist George Harrison took with him his unlikely-sounding Neoton Grazioso, a cheap Czech-made solidbody electric guitar probably better known by its British brandname, Futurama. A short time after the group's return from Germany, Harrison decided he needed something better. "We started making a bit of money," he later told *Guitar Player*, "because I saved up $120, and I saw an ad in the paper in Liverpool, and there was a guy selling his Gretsch Duo Jet." It turned out to be a sailor who had purchased the guitar in the US and brought it back to England. "It was my first real American guitar," Harrison recalled, "and I'll tell you, it was secondhand, but I polished that thing, I was so proud to own that."

Over the next few years The Beatles began their dramatic rise to fame, and Harrison continued to use his Duo Jet (pictured on pages 50-51) on the group's early recordings and gigs. By the time the band arrived in the US in February 1964 for their first concerts there and an appearance on Ed Sullivan's TV show, Harrison had moved onto a Gretsch Country Gentleman which he'd been using since the previous summer. "When we went to the States to play the *Ed Sullivan Show*, Gretsch gave me a [Country Gentleman] that I used on the show," said Harrison. "I read somewhere that after The Beatles appeared on that show Gretsch sold 20,000 guitars a week or something like that. I mean, we should have had shares..."

At first it seems surprising to look back and discover that Gretsch didn't make official contact with Harrison. But then The Beatles were caught in a whirlwind of success, and offers for marketing opportunities were surfacing from every entrepreneur with a Beatles wig or a plastic guitar to sell off the back of the mop-tops' success. In fact, Jimmie Webster made a promotional visit to Britain for Gretsch in April 1964 and intended to meet with Harrison while he was over. "There was supposed to be a meeting," recalls Webster's daughter Jennifer,

Gretsch on the box (right) This 1966 ad emphasized the huge exposure afforded Gretsch in the hands of The Monkees – but how many pre-pubescent female fans would actually buy a Gretsch guitar?

Monkees 1967 (below) The Monkees were a manufactured group targeting young teenagers via a regular TV show. Through a marketing deal they featured Gretsch instruments, and the company was quick to cash in on the connection by offering for sale an official Monkees guitar model. This red hollow body featured twin half-moon markers, Super'Tron humbuckers and prominent use of the group's logo.

The Monkees are selling Gretsch guitars and drums to 30 million teenagers watching network TV.

Need we say more?

*Just one thing more.
We're telling your customers about it
with advertisements in Boy's Life, Scholastic and
Hullabaloo to help sell more
Gretsch guitars and drums
for you.*

GRETSCH
THE FRED. GRETSCH MFG. CO.

© FRED. TRAVIS, DECEMBER, 1966

58

Pickguard (below) The Monkees guitar-shaped logo – looking suspiciously single-cutaway – appears on the white plastic pickguard.

music maker
JULY 1967

monkees report
burdon's hi-fi
price interview
art tatum 3s

Chet Atkins sleeve 1966 (above)
This LP of Beatles tunes features a cover
photo that partners four Beatle wigs
with a Gretsch 12-string guitar. The
instrument shown is in fact a prototype
that differs from the production version
in major ways, including position
markers, body, f-holes and color.

12-String 1966 (above) The 12-
string electric came to fame in the mid-
1960s and many guitar-making
companies produced their own versions
to try to get a share of a burgeoning
market. Gretsch was no exception, and
their twin-cutaway 12-String model
appeared in 1966. Apart from the
headstock, tailpiece and distinctive
triangle-shape position markers, much
of the 12-string was standard Gretsch
fare of the time, including the twin
Super'Tron humbucker pickups. The
model came in sunburst or natural, and
a fine example of the latter is shown
here. The July 1967 issue of 'Music
Maker' magazine (right) featured The
Monkees on the cover, as guitarist Mike
Nesmith poses with his natural finish
Gretsch 12-String model.

Position markers (below) Half-
moon markers appear on both sides of
the bound fingerboard.

Headstock (above) The headstock
carries a model nameplate as well as a
white plastic truss-rod cover bearing the
guitar-shaped Monkees logo.

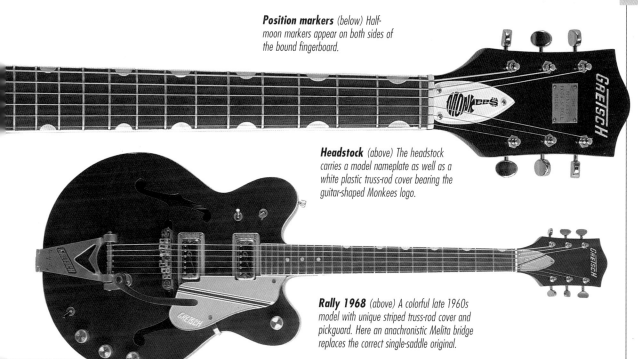

Rally 1968 (above) A colorful late 1960s
model with unique striped truss-rod cover and
pickguard. Here an anachronistic Melita bridge
replaces the correct single-saddle original.

"but it didn't happen. I don't think my father really cared that much personally," she laughs, "but he was willing to explore developing a guitar with him. And business had picked up when George used a Gretsch. My father was raving about that: 'Keep doing it, keep doing it,' he'd say, 'that's what we need!'"

During the middle 1960s there was a boom in the popularity of guitars, and the US industry hit a peak in 1965 with sales of around a million and a half instruments. Most of this was of course a result of the enormous growth in pop music, and a link to the biggest group of the time certainly did a company like Gretsch little harm. Thanks to Harrison and his highly visible Country Gents, business was good and the orders came flying in. "The guitar is truly the sound of the day," Jimmie Webster told a trade gathering in 1967.

Some organizational changes became necessary at Gretsch's New York headquarters to deal with this exceptional shift in the balance of their trade. One insider's estimate is that Gretsch had around 5000 back-orders for electric guitars stacking up at the time, and that for a customer to get one of the most popular models such as the Country Gentleman could mean a wait of over a year. Something had to change. Around 1966 the drum department was moved out of the Brooklyn factory to another location a few blocks away on South 5th Street, and a lot of the wholesaling operations were either stopped or moved to the Chicago office. All this was being done to allow the whole of the seventh floor at the factory to be turned over to guitar making.

Quality controller Dan Duffy, who by now had taken on more people such as Fred Rodriguez to cope with the increased demands on his department, remembers the changes well. "The transformation was amazing, totally mind boggling," he says. "If you could have seen the changes in that factory during the ten years since I started in 1956, well... You have to picture a company back in the 1950s trying to make 12 guitars a day, and possibly only getting out eight. In '66 we'd be aiming for 75, and some days we'd make 100 and more. We had racks made to hold 20 guitars, you'd see Country Gents, Anniversary models, White Falcons all lined up, 20 to a rack, being moving

throughout the factory. It was," says a nostalgic Duffy, "the most spectacular experience in my life."

MONKEE BUSINESS

During 1966 an American production company, Screen Gems, manufactured The Monkees pop group by hiring four actors and singers. The Monkees appeared that summer in a series of TV programs about the group's zany escapades, openly exploiting the success of The Beatles and in particular the style of their *Hard Day's Night* and *Help!* films.

Gretsch never had an actual 'signature' Beatles guitar, so perhaps they thought that a Monkees-endorsed model would be the next best thing. Phil Grant recalls: "Fred Gretsch Jr., Jimmie Webster and I went to a place in New York and watched some Monkees footage – they wanted us to sponsor the group with guitars and drums. I wasn't very enthusiastic about it. I've found that endorsements are only good if people look up to the fellow who's endorsing, if he's a real musician. The Monkees were a bunch of idiots: they were singers, and their playing was absolutely incidental to their act. So I said I'm not for it because they're not musicians, it's an insult to Chet Atkins and all the good drummers to say that these guys are Gretsch people. They were lousy musicians."

Grant was out-voted, and in 1966 Gretsch supplied instruments to the group, including the company's new 12-string guitar, a bass, a White Falcon, and a drum-kit. Gretsch then put its Monkees model onto the market, a red twin-cutaway thinline six-string emblazoned with Monkees guitar-shaped logos on truss-rod cover and pickguard. "We got letters from customers," remembers Dan Duffy, "and they'd say, 'Please send me a plain Gretsch pickguard and rod shield cover.' They didn't want the association of The Monkees on the guitar! We thought it was the best thing on the guitar, so attractive," he laughs, "and no one wanted it. They didn't want their guitar to be associated with The Monkees, maybe because they knew that the group didn't really play." The model never appeared in an official catalog or pricelist, and did not last much beyond 12 months in the Gretsch line.

GRETSCH FOR SALE

Shockwaves had been sent through the guitar manufacturing industry in 1965 when the Fender companies were sold to the Columbia Broadcasting System corporation for $13 million. It was by far and away the biggest sum ever paid for an instrument business, and other large companies began to look at the potential of the "expanding leisure-time market", as Fender's purchaser described it.

D H Baldwin, an Ohio-based musical instrument company specializing in the manufacture of pianos and organs, was actively seeking to purchase a guitar-making operation. In 1965 it had bid unsuccessfully for Fender. It then bought the Burns guitar company of England for $380,000, applying the Baldwin brandname to many existing Burns models. Baldwin's 1966 Annual Report described a rosy picture: for the first time in the company's long history overall sales exceeded $40 million, and for the fifth year sales and profits were up. There had been a decline in keyboard instrument sales, but "since guitars and amplifiers were introduced in the latter part of 1965, there were substantial increases over the figures of the previous year". Baldwin decided it could benefit further with a guitar brandname that had an existing high profile in the US... and turned its attention to Gretsch.

Every year Duke Kramer and Phil Grant, Gretsch vice-presidents based in Chicago and New York respectively, would go to dinner with Fred Gretsch Jr. on their return from the music trade fair in Frankfurt, Germany. Early in 1967, the dinner date with their 62 year-old boss came around. "We were back from a very successful fair," says Kramer, "and Fred drops this bomb on us that he was selling the company to Baldwin. It was a real shake-up." Grant recalls: "He mixed us a stiff drink each, and said, 'I have some news for you. I'm selling the company to Baldwin.' Well, we didn't know how to take it... and there was nothing much you could do about it."

Dick Harrison was Baldwin's treasurer at the time of the acquisition (later vice-president, then chief executive officer) and was involved in the negotiation and completion of the transaction, reporting to Baldwin's top man Morley Thompson who spearheaded the deal. Harrison outlines Fred Gretsch's reasons for selling: "I don't believe he had any offspring that was interested in pursuing the company; he had a young daughter, I believe, and that was all. I'm sure that he knew he had a company in an industry that was growing, and if he was ever going to diversify it would be a smart time to do that. I'm sure that's why he did it, and that's what he told me. Of course, we were dealing with a man who's giving up everything he owns in the way of a company, and naturally he wants to be careful how he does it. They were good negotiations with no major problems."

BALDWIN BUY-OUT

Plans for the sale were announced in May 1967, and *Music Trades* reported that "10,000 shares of Baldwin common stock and an undisclosed sum of cash" were involved. Some observers have since suggested an unofficial figure of $4 million. The report continued: "A new Baldwin subsidiary, organized to acquire these assets, will have Fred Gretsch as president. No change in the management of Gretsch is contemplated," adding: "Gretsch's sales in 1966 were in excess of $6 million. The acquisition of Gretsch will expand Baldwin's business in the guitar field and will put Baldwin in the drum and band instrument business."

It wasn't only the brandname and products that Baldwin considered valuable. It also recognized the worth of the most important name still associated with Gretsch guitars – Chet Atkins – and ensured this property remained secure. "I was important to that sale," explains Atkins, "because Mr. Gretsch came to me, said he was gonna sell to Baldwin, and asked me if I would sign a contract for so many years. I said, 'Why don't I get some stock?' And he wouldn't do it. I was real busy at the time, and I didn't have an attorney or anything, so I went ahead and signed it."

Overcoming their initial surprise, Gretsch personnel began to face their new future. Factory manager Bill Hagner says there were changes. "The Baldwin company were the greatest

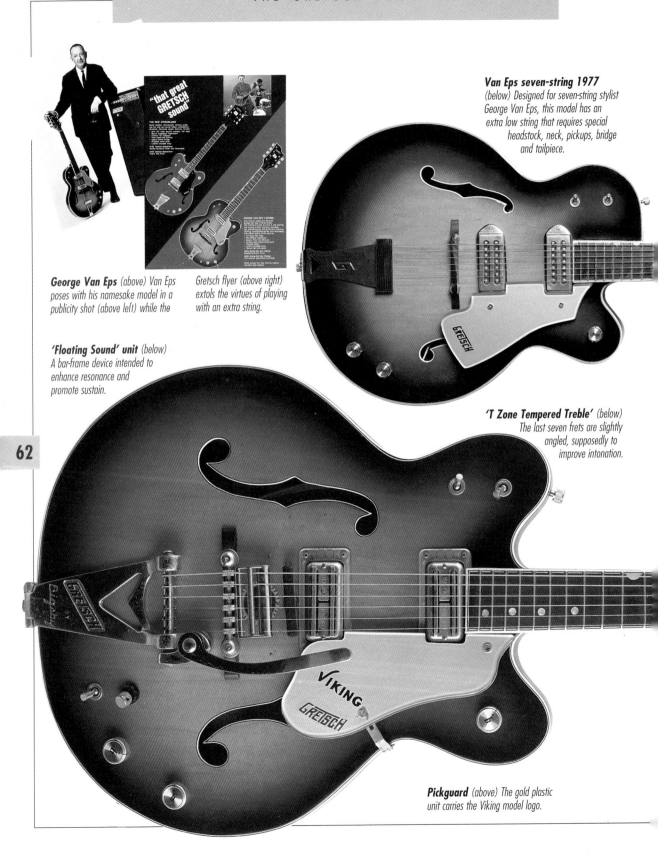

Van Eps seven-string 1977
(below) Designed for seven-string stylist
George Van Eps, this model has an
extra low string that requires special
headstock, neck, pickups, bridge
and tailpiece.

George Van Eps (above) Van Eps
poses with his namesake model in a
publicity shot (above left) while the

Gretsch flyer (above right)
extols the virtues of playing
with an extra string.

'Floating Sound' unit (below)
A bar-frame device intended to
enhance resonance and
promote sustain.

'T Zone Tempered Treble' (below)
The last seven frets are slightly
angled, supposedly to
improve intonation.

Pickguard (above) The gold plastic
unit carries the Viking model logo.

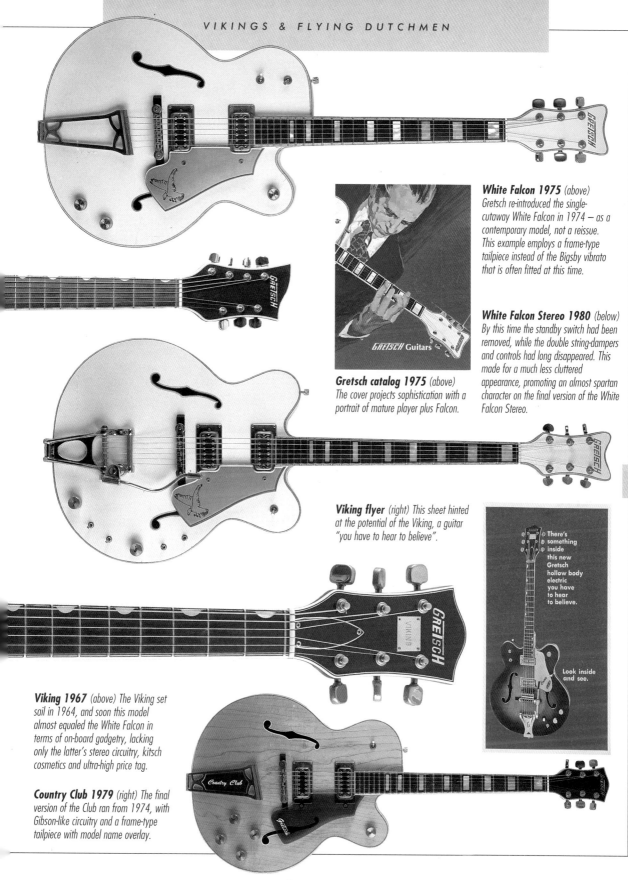

White Falcon 1975 (above)
Gretsch re-introduced the single-cutaway White Falcon in 1974 — as a contemporary model, not a reissue. This example employs a frame-type tailpiece instead of the Bigsby vibrato that is often fitted at this time.

White Falcon Stereo 1980 (below)
By this time the standby switch had been removed, while the double string-dampers and controls had long disappeared. This made for a much less cluttered appearance, promoting an almost spartan character on the final version of the White Falcon Stereo.

Gretsch catalog 1975 (above)
The cover projects sophistication with a portrait of mature player plus Falcon.

Viking flyer (right) This sheet hinted at the potential of the Viking, a guitar "you have to hear to believe".

Viking 1967 (above) The Viking set sail in 1964, and soon this model almost equaled the White Falcon in terms of on-board gadgetry, lacking only the latter's stereo circuitry, kitsch cosmetics and ultra-high price tag.

Country Club 1979 (right) The final version of the Club ran from 1974, with Gibson-like circuitry and a frame-type tailpiece with model name overlay.

63

manufacturing company of organs and pianos, but they tried to put their men into the guitar and drum business, and it wasn't the right thing to do. They had their own so-called engineers and so-called chemists and so-called this and that, and they wanted to incorporate their methods that they used in making pianos and organs. They said: 'Now we're going to do it this way,' and I would say, 'Wait a minute, we made that mistake 20 years ago.'"

Phil Grant reflects on Fred Gretsch Jr.'s motives for selling, and concludes, "I can't blame Fred, looking back on it now. But the usual thing happened: a company was bought up and the president promises nothing's going to change, your jobs are all secure, don't worry." Grant laughs: "And your check's in the mail. Anyway... I went along with it, and after a while you could see that things weren't going to be the way that you hoped they would be. Baldwin would press a button, say, 'Let's do it this way,' and anybody's personal feelings never entered into their decisions at all."

ALL THE WAY TO ARKANSAS

Baldwin was disappointed with the business results of the merger. "When you put two companies together you like to believe that one plus one equals three," says Dick Harrison. "If you have a sales force out there that would be capable of selling Gretsch guitars in addition to Baldwin pianos, that would have represented some synergy, in other words you would come out better by having done it. But the products were so different, and we felt that it would have been a great mistake to put the Gretsch guitar in the hands of our Baldwin sales people, so we never did that.

"Another example of synergy would have been if our factories that make pianos, primarily woodworking operations, could make guitars. Again, they're so different that that didn't come about.

"Gretsch did well for a while," concludes Harrison, "but then the industry turned down and of course that hurt us. I would say that it really wasn't a financial success for us. And that certainly wasn't the fault of anybody from Gretsch; that

was as much the industry's fault and our fault as anything else." Baldwin had begun to diversify away from its original core of music and into financial services, including banking and insurance. The company's Annual Report for 1969 noted a 12 per cent drop in Gretsch sales, conveniently attributing over half the fall to a three-month strike that began in October 1969.

By the following year plans were underway to move the Gretsch factory out of its 54 year-old home in Brooklyn to a site in Booneville, Arkansas, well over 1000 miles away, where Baldwin already operated a number of factories and enjoyed cheaper and more amenable labor. Of course, the move did not please an already disgruntled workforce, and very few personnel made the move south-west in late summer 1970. The Brooklyn building continued to house the Gretsch sales office until that too was moved, first to the Chicago office and then to Baldwin's HQ in Cincinnati, Ohio, and so by the summer of 1972 the last Gretsch connection with number 60 Broadway, Brooklyn, had been severed.

One of the few who relocated to the Booneville site was factory manager Bill Hagner. "I moved everything down and set it up, and I taught the new people what to do and how to do it. That lasted several years. The factory was a big converted barn up on top of the mountain about five miles out of a small town of 3000 people. You had to take people off the farms and try to teach them how to work. When you're used to New York, well... You move down there and they'd be polishing a guitar for four hours instead of a half hour." Hagner lasted at Booneville until 1972 when he was moved to Baldwin's Ohio offices to work with the sales force.

Some of the old names remained: Fred Gretsch Jr. became a Baldwin board member, for example, and Duke Kramer went to Cincinnati in 1972 as Gretsch's general sales manager. Of the many who departed when the move was made, Dan Duffy left in 1970, at first going back to full-time playing and teaching, and then on to positions in various musical instrument companies, while Phil Grant left in 1972 to set up a grocery business in Vermont. Jimmie Webster made some Guitarama-style appearances for Gretsch after the sale to Baldwin, but gradually drifted away from the guitar company that he had done so much to establish and worked so hard to promote. Webster died in 1978 at the age of 69.

Chet Atkins, who since the 1980s has had a deal with the Gibson company, offers a concise recollection of the Gretsch/Baldwin set-up: "They just couldn't build Gretsch guitars at Booneville. I complained, and they hired a man called Dean Porter, he moved to Arkansas and got the guitars so they would play. But the quality never was like it was in Brooklyn," Atkins suggests.

BALDWIN'S BURNS BOOST

Just before the Baldwin buy-out, Gretsch's pricelist of November 1966 had detailed 15 electrics in the line. There were 11 archtops: the Clipper at $200; Anniversary one-pickup at $245; Anniversary two-pickup $300; Chet Atkins Tennessean $400; Country Club $475 (sunburst; natural $500); Chet Atkins Hollow Body $500; 12-string $500; Chet Atkins Country Gentleman $650; Viking $675 (sunburst or Cadillac Green; natural $700); White Falcon $900; and White Falcon Stereo $1000. There were four solids: the Corvette two-pickup at $265; Astro-Jet $350; Duo Jet $375 (including color sparkle options); and Jet Fire Bird $375.

The first catalog issued after Baldwin took over in 1967 highlighted the return of Bigsby vibratos to the solidbody models, as well as the first new Gretsch model of the Baldwin era, the $395 Rally. This was a twin-cutaway thinline archtop, unusual in that it featured a built-in active treble-boost circuit, which was also added to the Corvette at this time. (The circuit may have been derived from Baldwin's Burns connection, as the UK company had pioneered the use of active circuitry in the early 1960s.) Quite why Gretsch wanted to boost the treble of a guitar already equipped with trebly HiLo'Tron single-coil pickups is unknown.

Definitely borrowed from Baldwin's Burns-originated guitars was the 'gear box' method of truss-rod adjustment, accessed through the back of the body at the neck heel. Gretsch began to incorporate this on its instruments during the early 1970s, coincidentally following the cessation of Baldwin/Burns instrument production in Britain. Under Baldwin, Gretsch also decided to allow air into its 'sealed' archtops by reviving real, open f-holes on the bodies from about 1972.

SEVEN SILVER STRINGS

Before production moved in 1970 from Brooklyn to Booneville there was a period when Gretsch made a number of limited-run instruments for various retailers, players, teachers and so on. Not that Gretsch had ever been shy of custom work, most famously exemplified by the handful of odd-shaped solids they made for Bo Diddley around 1960. An insider explains: "Gretsch was always small enough to be flexible, and always tried to fill small niches in the business. That's why nobody can nail down what Gretsch did on a particular model, because maybe 10 per cent of our business was custom guitars. If someone wanted a pink guitar with blue stripes, we made it. If somebody wanted a guitar with a narrow neck at the nut, we made it. It cost the customer extra money, but we were small enough to be able to do that."

Small-order batches in the 1960s included specially modified models for Gretsch dealers such as Sam Ash (Anniversary-style with cat's-eye shape soundholes), Sam Goody (twin-cutaway archtop with 'G' soundholes), and Sherman Clay (gold- and silver-finish Corvettes, later nicknamed 'Silver Duke' and 'Gold Duke'). Our insider continues: "Dealers liked the idea of an exclusive instrument because they could point to it and say no one else has it, and they could charge a certain amount of dollars and know that nobody could quote a cheaper price." Special small-run 'signature' guitars were also made, including a limited number for New York-based player/teacher/store-owner Ronny Lee, as well as some six- and seven-string models named for guitarist George Van Eps (the seven-string version of which remained in the catalog for ten years).

Van Eps had become well known for big band work from the 1930s, and after World War II he'd moved to the West Coast and successfully concentrated on film studio work. In the

Super Chet 1972 (below) The large and ornate Super Chet model was introduced in 1972, a distinctive feature being the controls mounted along the edge of the pickguard. This early example has been modified by owner Chet Atkins, the original selector on the left upper bout replaced by a complex array of eight mini-switches.

Tailpiece (above) A frame-type tailpiece carries an ebony insert with some fancy abalone inlay work.

Pickguard (above) This carries three volume and two tone controls.

Gretsch catalog 1972 (left) This brochure for the Atkins models features a Super Chet headstock on the cover.

Hi Roller 1978 (right) With its distinctive dice-style position markers, the Hi Roller was originally made in 1976, effectively as a prototype to the subsequent Atkins Axe and Super Axe models. Intriguingly, this Hi Roller dates from two years later, and it features differences to the earlier type that suggest it was a custom-order one-off.

GRETSCH Guitars
Chet Atkins Models

66

Country Gentleman custom 1967 (below) Gretsch built this scaled-down Country Gentleman (Gentleboy?) specially for Chet Atkins, complete with full-size f-holes.

Chet Atkins sleeve 1972 (above) The cover of this LP, 'Finger Pickin Good', has a fine shot displaying the two Chets: Atkins and Super.

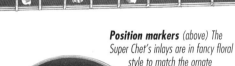

Position markers (above) The Super Chet's inlays are in fancy floral style to match the ornate headstock work.

Super Chet ad (right) Around 1973, Chet Atkins praises his new Super Chet model. Does he look to you like a man about to wield a soldering iron and eight mini-switches?

"It's the best there is." *Chet Atkins*

The Gretsch **Super Chet.**

RCA Studios, Nashville, Tennessee

GRETSCH

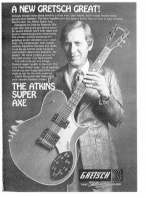

A NEW GRETSCH GREAT!

THE ATKINS SUPER AXE

GRETSCH
THAT GREAT GRETSCH SOUND!

Chet Atkins' Super Axe 1977 (above) Launched in '77, this large but slim-bodied solid featured an array of on-board active effects modules spanning phase, compression and sustain, with all the appropriate controls on an elliptical panel. According to Gretsch's ad from 1977 (left), Chet designed this new model and obviously liked what he heard as a result, stating: "In all modesty I think my new Super Axe is the ultimate guitar for the rock musician." Unfortunately, the latter chose not to share his opinion.

1940s the Epiphone company had built him a custom guitar based on his unusual requirement for a seven-string model, adding a low-A below the existing E-string (over 40 years before Steve Vai came up with a similar idea). Van Eps once explained that the reason for the additional low A-string was based on his love of deep basslines, and because he approached the guitar as "a complete instrument within itself", almost a mini-orchestra. Gretsch produced Van Eps single-cutaway models from 1968, in six-string ($575) as well as seven-string ($675) versions, underlining again the company's flexible approach, enabling the manufacture of small numbers of limited-appeal instruments – even if it did mean tooling-up for the unique 14-pole humbuckers necessary for the seven-string.

Of course, Gretsch was still keeping an eye on its major models, as well as habitually monitoring Gibson's marketing moves. In the late 1960s, guitarists had begun to rediscover Gibson's old Les Paul models, and finally in 1968 Gibson re-introduced its early-style single-cutaway design for which almost everyone seemed to be clamoring. Gretsch responded by bringing back *its* discontinued single-cutaway solidbody design, last seen in 1961. It launched the $350 Roc Jet in 1969, and shortly afterwards its remaining twin-cutaway Jet models were grounded.

FUSSING WITH THE SUPER CHET

One can imagine the thought crossing Baldwin's mind that as it had a contract ensuring Chet Atkins' involvement with Gretsch for a number of years, it may as well exploit it. In 1972 a new Gretsch Chet Atkins design hit the market in the shape of two broadly similar models, the Deluxe Chet and the Super Chet.

The big, deep-bodied, single-cutaway archtop style was the result of a collaboration between Chet Atkins, Dean Porter and Clyde Edwards. Porter was described by Gretsch as their 'master technician' (and as Atkins has already told us was the man who "got the guitars so they would play"), while Edwards was Gretsch's 'master string instrument designer'. A company

newsletter of the time says, "The surest way of getting this super guitar was to turn these three men loose and tell them to design the best guitar they could, no holds barred... More fussing went into this guitar than you can imagine."

A lot of the fussing must have been spent on the large amount of decorative work employed on the Super Chet, which had flowery inlays sprouting on the fingerboard, headstock and tailpiece. It also sported an unusual row of control 'wheels' built into the pickguard's edge. The Deluxe Chet was a plainer version, with conventional controls and none of the foliage, and did not last long. The Super Chet, which stayed in the line for some seven years, was also decorated with an attractive inlaid center stripe around the body sides. Atkins was responsible for this, as he explains: "I had a little acoustic guitar from the 1800s that a lady had given me, it had a lot of inlay on it and inlay in the center of the sides, so I had them do that. We were trying to make a really beautiful guitar, Clyde just tried to build the prettiest guitar ever."

The August 1972 pricelist shows 14 electric models in the Gretsch line, of which 13 are archtops: the Clipper at $250; Anniversary two-pickup at $345; Streamliner $395 (a lower-price twin-cutaway archtop launched in 1968); Chet Atkins Tennessean $495; Country Club $500 (sunburst; natural $525); Chet Atkins Nashville $595 (this had been the Hollow Body's new name since about 1967); Van Eps seven-string $675; Chet Atkins Country Gentleman $695; Viking $700 (sunburst; natural $725); Deluxe Chet $750; Super Chet $850; White Falcon $975; and White Falcon Stereo $1100. The solitary solid was the Roc Jet at $395 (in red, orange or black; $425 in brown).

BOLT-ON NECKS, TUMBLING DICE

The odd Gretsch Roc II appeared in 1973. It was a single-cutaway solid with an elliptical control plate carrying circuitry intended to produce copious quantities of treble and distortion. "High degree of treble booster for 'screaming' rock sounds," said the publicity. "No thank you," said most guitarists.

Following on from 1969's Roc Jet, which was partly prompted by a growing sense of nostalgia for older-style instruments, Gretsch added the Country Roc to the line in 1974, a Western-appointed solidbody which evoked the company's Round Up model of the 1950s. In the same year it re-introduced a single-cutaway deep-body mono White Falcon, a model last made with this kind of body shape some 12 years earlier. The 'new' Falcon partnered the contemporary twin-cutaway thinline mono and stereo versions.

Two new downscale guitars came along in 1975, the Broadkaster solidbody and semi-hollow electrics. As usual Gretsch was to some extent following Gibson's lead – and on this occasion the path was an unpopular one. Gibson had launched the Marauder, its first solidbody guitar with a Fender-style bolt-on neck, in 1974; likewise, the Broadkaster solid was the first Gretsch with a bolt-on neck, while it also displayed strong Stratocaster styling influences. Neither of these new Gretsch guitars drew much praise, and the Broadkasters sat at the bottom of their respective categories on the pricelist.

Under the Dorado brandname, Baldwin had added a Japanese-made solidbody electric to its catalog around 1972, separate from Gretsch but significant in that it was the first dealing with oriental guitar manufacturing. The connection brought dividends four years later when a Japanese supplier was chosen to provide new pickups for several Gretsch models. Ray Butts' patent for the Filter'Tron pickup reached the end of its official 17-year run in 1976, and the previous year he'd received a letter from Gretsch advising that royalty payments would end. Butts recalls: "I had made a handshake agreement on my humbucking pickup with Mr. Gretsch. He told me they'd done business that way with K Zildjian in Turkey, the cymbal manufacturers, for over 50 years, and also with Cuesnon band instruments in France. So we had no written agreement, which was fine at the time.

"When the company was sold," Butts continues, "Baldwin just sort of forgot about everything. With that letter in '75 they sent me a little money, and said they felt the agreement no longer applied." In the letter, Gretsch also asked Butts if he might devise a new pickup for possible use on the Roc Jet and

Broadkaster models, and on the "new Chet Atkins Hi-Roller model guitar". When Butts understandably declined, Gretsch turned to a Japanese supplier, and soon began fitting cheap-quality 'humbuckers' (which perform suspiciously like single-coils) to the existing Roc Jet and Broadkasters.

As for the 'Atkins Hi-Roller', this was the original name given to a model that evolved into the new Super Axe and Atkins Axe guitars of 1977. Gretsch were still hazy about a name late in 1976, confirmed by an ad which mentioned an upcoming instrument to be called the 'Atkins Yakety Axe'. The distinctive look of these big new solidbody guitars with their sweeping, pointed cutaway was the subject of a patent issued to Gretsch designer Clyde Edwards for its "ornamental design". Also involved were Chet Atkins, and Gretsch general manager Duke Kramer.

Kramer recalls: "Chet wanted to call it the Hi-Roller guitar, and he wanted to put on dice as position markers. We made a few with the dice, we even had it down as the Hi-Roller on a pricelist, but the Baldwin people thought the name and the dice gave the guitar a bad connotation of gambling, and they didn't want that. So we left the markers plain, and we called it the Super Axe. Chet wanted more sustain, so he put on a compressor, and he wanted a phaser on it, both of which the Baldwin engineers came up with."

When the two models were launched, the effects-laden version was called the Super Axe and the less expensive gadget-less option the Atkins Axe – despite the fact that Atkins had originated the idea for the built-in electronic effects. Nonetheless, Atkins appeared in Gretsch's ads at the time pushing the Super Axe, which was clearly the version he liked. Some of this confusion may have arisen because Gretsch had also become interested in an endorsement from country guitarist Roy Clark.

Kramer says that it was decided not to put Chet Atkins' name on the guitars. "We were going to pay Chet a royalty because he helped design it, but we weren't going to have his name. I took the guitar out to Roy Clark, and he fell in love with it. He wanted to play it, and I said OK, we might make it the Roy Clark model.

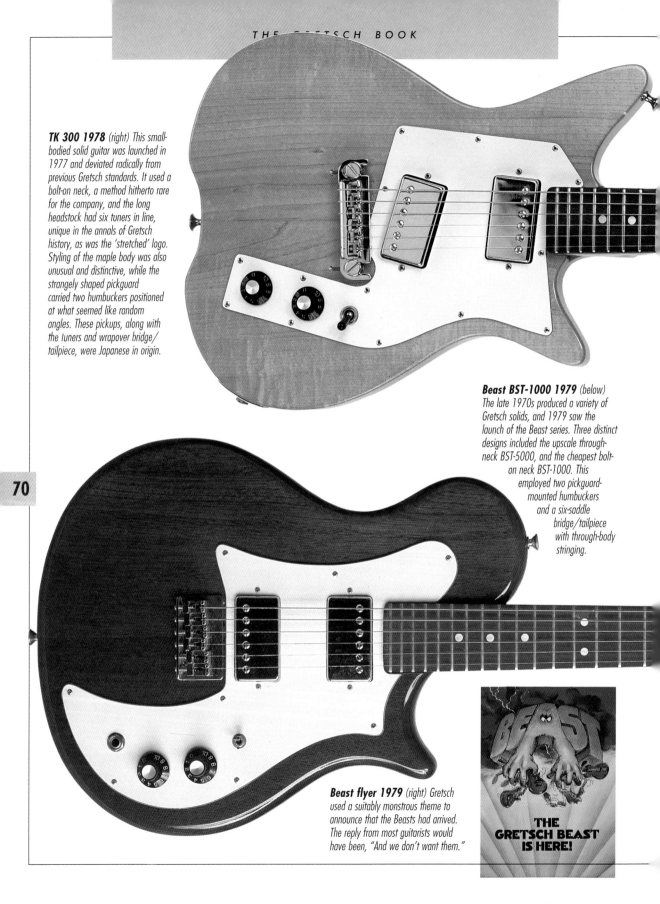

TK 300 1978 (right) This small-bodied solid guitar was launched in 1977 and deviated radically from previous Gretsch standards. It used a bolt-on neck, a method hitherto rare for the company, and the long headstock had six tuners in line, unique in the annals of Gretsch history, as was the 'stretched' logo. Styling of the maple body was also unusual and distinctive, while the strangely shaped pickguard carried two humbuckers positioned at what seemed like random angles. These pickups, along with the tuners and wrapover bridge/tailpiece, were Japanese in origin.

Beast BST-1000 1979 (below) The late 1970s produced a variety of Gretsch solids, and 1979 saw the launch of the Beast series. Three distinct designs included the upscale through-neck BST-5000, and the cheapest bolt-on neck BST-1000. This employed two pickguard-mounted humbuckers and a six-saddle bridge/tailpiece with through-body stringing.

70

Beast flyer 1979 (right) Gretsch used a suitably monstrous theme to announce that the Beasts had arrived. The reply from most guitarists would have been, "And we don't want them."

THE GRETSCH BEAST IS HERE!

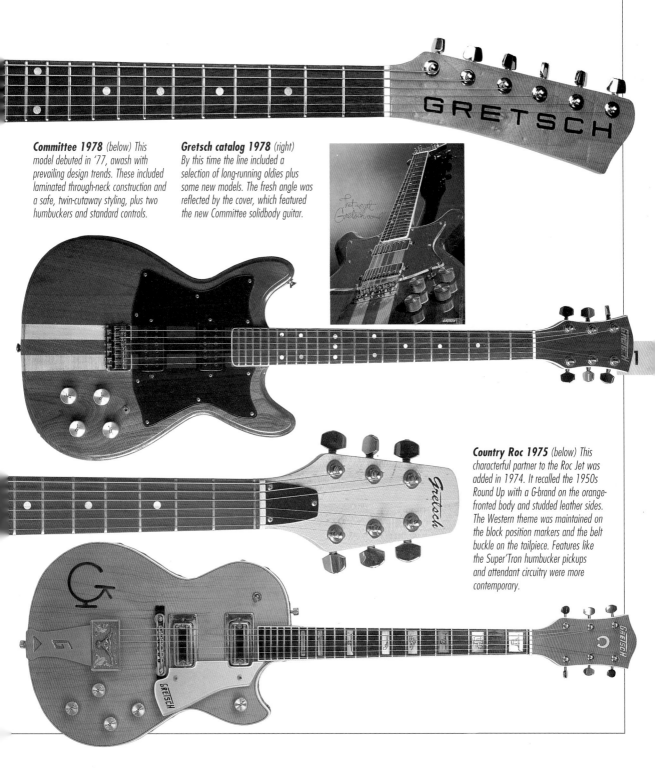

Committee 1978 (below) This model debuted in '77, awash with prevailing design trends. These included laminated through-neck construction and a safe, twin-cutaway styling, plus two humbuckers and standard controls.

Gretsch catalog 1978 (right) By this time the line included a selection of long-running oldies plus some new models. The fresh angle was reflected by the cover, which featured the new Committee solidbody guitar.

Country Roc 1975 (below) This characterful partner to the Roc Jet was added in 1974. It recalled the 1950s Round Up with a G-brand on the orange-fronted body and studded leather sides. The Western theme was maintained on the block position markers and the belt buckle on the tailpiece. Features like the Super'Tron humbucker pickups and attendant circuitry were more contemporary.

He said that'd be great. I got back and told Chet, and he didn't like that at all, so we never did it – although Roy did use and play the guitar, and we did some advertising with him."

MEET THE BEAST FAMILY

There were a couple more solidbody electrics added to the Gretsch line in 1977, the TK 300 and the Committee. The TK 300 was another cheap bolt-on-neck solid, this time with a strange, asymmetric body, while the Committee followed a trend of the time for through-neck construction, where the neck travels the complete length of the guitar and added 'wings' complete the body shape. But these were uninspiring guitars by any standards, and appeared to be almost totally lacking in the character which had once been at the heart of Gretsch design.

A pricelist from April 1977 sums up the Gretsch line of 18 electrics. There were 11 archtops: the Broadkaster at $495 (sunburst or natural, or $550 with vibrato; red $525); Anniversary two-pickup $625; Chet Atkins Tennessean $695; Country Club $725 (Antique Maple; natural $750); Chet Atkins Nashville $795; Van Eps seven-string $795; Chet Atkins Country Gentleman $895; White Falcon single-cutaway $1050; Super Chet $1150 (with vibrato $1200); White Falcon twin-cutaway mono $1175; and White Falcon twin-cutaway stereo $1295. There were seven solids: the TK 300 at $325; Broadkaster at $450; Committee $495; Country Roc $695; Atkins Axe $750; and Super Axe $895.

The last new Gretsch guitars to appear under Baldwin ownership were the Beast solids, launched in 1979. These came in a number of styles, with a single-cutaway body akin to a scaled-down Super Axe, as well as a couple of twin-cutaway types. Gretsch seemed to want to be all things to all guitarists with the Beasts, absorbing design elements from Gibson, Fender and contemporary Japanese makers. "All the sound you can ask for," boasted a promotional leaflet. "New pickups, new electronics, completely new designs make it all happen."

The Beast series ranged in price from $299.50 for a one-pickup bolt-on-neck model to $695 for a two-pickup through-neck guitar. If anything, the Beasts seemed functional rather than inspirational, and although few people realized at the time – "this is only the beginning of what you can expect from the Beast family" said the optimistic ad – they were to be the last gasp from Gretsch in the 1970s, and as such marked the end of an era with a depressingly low note.

THE MACHINES STOP

If Baldwin's performance in handling their fresh acquisition was measured by the aptitude and success of the new Gretsch models it launched in the 1970s, then the score would be low. As we shall see, it fared little better in the business affairs surrounding Gretsch.

The sequence of events is difficult to establish with complete accuracy, but this is what seems to have happened. Although sales picked up a little for Gretsch in the early 1970s, Baldwin was still not seeing a profit from the business, despite the various cost-cutting exercises that had been undertaken.

In early 1973 there was a bad fire at the factory, adding to the negative picture, and Baldwin decided to contract the manufacture of Gretsch products to long-standing factory manager Bill Hagner. He formed the Hagner Musical Instrument Corp for the purpose, still operating from the Booneville site. "They didn't want to be bothered with it any more," remembers Hagner, "and assuming that I knew what I was doing they decided to take a chance and do it that way." Another fire at the end of 1973 did not help these new plans.

At the very start of 1976, Hagner opened a revitalized factory at Booneville, an event reported at the time as a "re-opening" with the building described as "a spanking new plant affirming Gretsch plans to grow". This implies that production may not have been great during 1974 and 1975. The Hagner manufacturing deal ceased at the end of 1978, when control passed back fully to Baldwin.

In early 1979, Baldwin bought the Kustom amplifier company, and by the end of the year had merged Gretsch with Kustom, moving the sales and administration office for the new combined operation to Chanute, Kansas.

It was probably some time in 1980 that Baldwin finally decided that it would stop production of Gretsch guitars, and it seems that very little new product was manufactured beyond the start of 1981 (just short of the 100th anniversary). Gretsch drums continued to be made at Booneville until '81, when the business was transferred to a Baldwin factory in De Queen, Arkansas, about 80 miles south of Booneville, and later to Texarkana, Arkansas, even further south. Charlie Roy was running the Gretsch/Kustom operation, and bought it from Baldwin in early 1982, when the offices were moved to Gallatin, Tennessee, just outside Nashville. By now Chet Atkins' endorsement deal had come to a natural end, and he soon transferred allegiance to Gibson (who began making a Chet Atkins Country Gentleman model in 1987).

Roy appears to have continued selling existing Gretsch guitar stock as late as 1983. The last Kustom/Gretsch pricelist we have seen is dated from January of that year and shows only Committee and Beast models, presumably left-overs. Baldwin again took control of the Gretsch company in about 1984, when the deal with Roy ceased. Around this time there was a last-ditch plan to revive Gretsch guitar production at a Baldwin piano-action factory in Ciudad Juarez, Mexico, but most observers agree that only a small trial batch was assembled, after which the idea was dropped.

FRED GRETSCH (SLIGHT RETURN)

Dick Harrison, who had become chief executive officer at Baldwin in 1972, explains that his company, now officially known as Baldwin United, was undergoing dramatic changes in the late 1970s. "By the early 1980s it had become predominantly a financial services company, and the music was always doing well but was a very small part of the total." Baldwin's musical strength was in the piano and organ business, he emphasizes, and says that despite all the efforts it never did well with Gretsch guitars, amplifiers and drums. "Baldwin United went bankrupt in September 1983. Out of that, the music company was purchased by myself and another gentleman, and we completed the deal by June of 1984," explains Harrison.

The new Baldwin Piano & Organ Co then proceeded to sell Kustom, after which it turned its attention to Gretsch... and this is when yet another Fred Gretsch comes into the picture. It wasn't Fred Gretsch Jr. – he had died at the age of 75 in 1980 – but one of his nephews, whom we shall call Fred Gretsch III.

Fred III had originally worked at Gretsch from 1965 to 1971, starting in product engineering and working on the factory expansion around 1966. "I'd been going to the Brooklyn factory since about 1951 when Fred Sr., my grandfather, took me there as quite a young fellow," says Fred III. "I probably started going there at five years old. I credit him with activating in me quite a good interest in the business." Fred III explains how he felt when his uncle, Fred Jr., sold out to Baldwin in 1967. "I was personally disappointed because I was working in the business, and it was my long term ambition to own it myself one day. But that was going to take another 17 years to achieve."

GRETSCH REVIVAL

When he left Gretsch in 1971, Fred Gretsch III began his own musical instrument importing and wholesaling business, and acquired the Synsonics brand in 1980 from Mattel, which led to some success with acoustic and electronic percussion as well as electric guitars. "I saw Dick Harrison regularly at trade shows and I would mention to him my interest in buying the Gretsch business if it ever came up for sale. I guess I kept an eye on the bankruptcy of the Baldwin financial parent. At that point they brought Duke Kramer in to run the Gretsch business again, taking it back from Charlie Roy, and I just kept up with Duke. Between the two of us we figured that they were ready to sell it. Negotiations began and were ultimately successful in November of 1984, and I bought the business in January of '85," says Fred III.

"The plan was to continue drum making in Arkansas for a year, then to move it to our location in South Carolina, and subsequently to get the guitar business going again. Duke Kramer was an important contributor to the program of

73

Traveling Wilburys TW-500
1989 (right) This was one of a line of inexpensive models of Korean origin produced to tie in with the promotion for The Traveling Wilburys, a fictitious group composed of famous names hiding behind Wilbury aliases. The 1989 ad (below) shows members Bob Dylan, Jeff Lynne, Tom Petty, Roy Orbison and George Harrison, plus a guitar adorned with travel graphics.

IT'S OFFICIAL!

THE GENUINE, AUTHORIZED WILBURY GUITAR • IN THREE SIGNED MODEL DESIGNED BY OTIS, NELSON & CHARLIE T. W

"THE GUITAR WITH THE SIGNATURES ON EACH GUITAR WITH IT'S OWN "ORIGINAL GRA

FRED GRETSCH ENTERPRI

RIDGELAND, S.C.   P.O. BOX 358 • 29
(803) 726-6144   FAX (803) 726-8143   Tele

Brian Setzer ad 1994 (above) Long-time Gretsch fan and erstwhile Stray Cat, Setzer conceded that old is not necessarily best, and supplied design ideas for a Japanese-made signature model based on the existing Nashville. Ecstatic about the end result, he happily endorsed his new Gretsch (although the Japanese copywriter had problems with Setzer's name).

Nashville Brian Setzer 1994
(right) The Nashville 6120-1960 model of 1992 re-created some of the aspects of an original 1960 Chet Atkins Hollow Body model. Features such as half-moon markers, zero fret, horseshoe headstock logo, Filter'Tron humbucker pickups, and three controls plus two selectors help to place it in the correct historical context. The Setzer version discards the zero fret and adds appropriate signature and model logos. Optional dice-style control knobs complete the Setzer's spec, and the model comes with vintage lacquer finish option. The standard color is orange (right), but green (above) is another colorful alternative that was added to the line in 1995, available on the Nashville since 1993.

Blue Pearl Sparkle Jet 1995
(right) We'll overlook Gretsch's
contrary description of this guitar
(pearl and sparkle together?) and
note that a new migration is underway
from Gretsch drum finishes to guitar bodies.

Gretsch catalog 1990 (above)
This was the first Gretsch guitar
catalog for the brand newly
revived in the 1980s, the
cover portraying an example
of the new Japanese-made
models in a sepia-tinted
vintage light.

Duo Jet 6128/Silver Jet (above) Two mid-1990s
examples from the current Jet family: the black Duo Jet
recreates a 1957 version – note narrow headstock, single-coil
pickups – contrasting the Silver Jet.

**Country Classic II 6122-1962
1994** (above) The Country Classic II
6122, despite being something of a
mouthful, recalls nothing less than the
twin-cutaway Chet Atkins Country
Gentleman. The 1962 suffix signifies the
original period of inspiration: zero fret, fake
f-holes, three controls and three selectors,
and a single-saddle bridge. These are the
features that differ from those found on the
standard version of the 6122.

Gretsch ad 1993 (above) This
Japanese promo uses an eye-
catching trio of headstocks
(Nashville, Country Classic,
Anniversary) to draw attention
to new models that were
appearing in the current
Gretsch line.

bringing the guitars back, and without his hard work, enthusiasm and energy it would have been impossible."

Kramer says that they decided to introduce updated versions of the classic Gretsch models of the past, and no doubt they had noticed the increasing prices that certain Gretsch guitars were fetching on the 'vintage' market. Kramer drew up specifications for the proposed new models, going to long-time Gretsch suppliers such as Jasper Wood Products and Bigsby in the US as well as to new people like hardware manufacturer Müller of Germany.

Then Kramer and Gretsch had to find someone to produce the guitars. Kramer visited many American makers: "I went to the Heritage factory, I went to the Guild factory, we even petitioned Gibson, would they assemble these guitars for us?" But negotiations with US makers were not successful. "So then our only option was to go offshore," explains Kramer, "and I went to Japan and selected Terada. They were used to making hollow body guitars, whereas the rest were used to making mainly solidbody guitars. And the instruments we're getting from over there now are absolutely gorgeous. I hate to say this, but from a playing standpoint they're much better than the old ones were," he laughs.

OLD BOTTLES, NEW MEDICINE

In 1989 Gretsch offered an unusual forerunner to its forthcoming guitars with a series of Korean-made electrics intended to capitalize on the popularity of the Traveling Wilburys. This was a fictional family supergroup composed of George Harrison ('Nelson Wilbury'), Jeff Lynne ('Otis'), Bob Dylan ('Lucky'), Tom Petty ('Charlie T Jr.') and Roy Orbison ('Lefty'). The cheap and somewhat primitive guitars were loosely based on the group's old Danelectro instruments, and various models were issued, all boldly finished in what Gretsch called their "original graphics" with an appropriate travel-associated theme.

Fred Gretsch Enterprises Ltd. delivered its first proper Gretsch guitars to dealers by the second half of 1989. Obviously it could no longer use Chet Atkins' name, and while some of the model names were necessarily modified, others were more familiar. The September 1989 pricelist showed nine electric models. There were five archtops: the Tennessee Rose at $1495 (recalling a Tennessean); the Nashville at $1750; Nashville Western at $1875 (with G-brand and Western appointments); Country Classic single-cutaway at $1975 (recalling a Country Club); and the Country Classic twin-cutaway at $1975 (recalling a Country Gent). There were four solids: the Duo Jet at $1300; Silver Jet at $1400; Jet Firebird $1400; and Round Up $1550. This initial selection was soon joined by a pair of White Falcon models in single- or twin-cutaway styles.

Since then the revitalized Gretsch operation has, like so many of its contemporaries, placed increasing emphasis on revisiting the past. This has resulted in the reissue of various oldies that bear re-activated pickup and hardware designs, including the reincarnation of Filter'Tron humbucker and DeArmond single-coil pickups. The company also recently launched a 'signature' model from one of the best known modern players of Gretsch, Brian Setzer, whose rockabilly work with the Stray Cats and subsequent solo ventures have provided an apposite contemporary setting for those familiar Gretsch tones, suitably celebrated in an attractive new model.

Since the first crop of new models in 1989, Gretsch has added several more guitars, including a Black Falcon, an Anniversary reissue and a variety of fresh color options, as well as a series for sale only in Japan that revives the old Electromatic name. The latest venture at the time of writing is a US-made line of selected 'Custom USA' classics, and with this return to American manufacturing sources the Gretsch electric guitar has come full circle.

The last word goes to Dan Duffy, quality controller at Gretsch for many years from the late 1950s. "You go into a guitar store and you buy a name," he says. "But if only you realized what went into that guitar, all the lives and the years that guys took to make those guitars the way they were. And it wasn't Fred Gretsch Jr., as much as we loved him: it was the guys who got there every morning at six o'clock. They did it. You remember that."

REFERENCE SECTION

There are five parts within the reference section that takes up the rest of this book. Starting on page 78 is the MODEL IDENTIFICATION INDEX, explained below. A key to MODEL NUMBERS is on page 82/3. The main REFERENCE LISTING begins on page 86, and how best to use it is covered on page 84/5. Methods for DATING Gretsch guitars, including all-important serial number tables, can be found on page 102/3. Closing the reference section on page 104/5 is a CHRONOLOGY showing all Gretsch electric guitar models in the order that they were introduced.

As with any brand, and perhaps even more so with Gretsch, there are exceptions to any 'rules' – watch out for custom-order instruments, factory prototypes, anachronistic transitional variants and examples modified by owners, for example. But this reference section should enable you to determine these differences from the Gretsch norm.

THE MODEL IDENTIFICATION INDEX, which commences overleaf and continues to page 81, is designed to help you quickly and simply distinguish between Gretsch models. Many do carry an appropriate name on the headstock or pickguard, and if this easy ID aspect is present then look it up in the index (page 106/7) where the *italic* page number will indicate the main Reference Listing.

Most Gretsches also have a four-digit model code (not to be confused with the serial number) which usually appears on a label attached somewhere within the body. This model number can determine the identity of an instrument – see the Model Numbers chart on page 82/3. However, if you can see neither name nor number then other recognition methods must be used.

A major clue is provided by the body shape, and for Gretsch there are 20 distinctively different designs, which we have chosen to call STYLES, each allocated a number and relevant silhouette. Under every style on the next few pages is a list of the guitars employing that body outline, and each entry provides further identification pointers in the form of easily spotted comparative features. This is followed by the Gretsch model designation, production period, and a page number showing where to look in the main Reference Listing for more detailed information.

By first matching a guitar to the correct body silhouette and then checking the identification features listed under the appropriate style heading, it should be possible to ascertain the model and find its entry in the main Reference Listing. To differentiate Japanese-made models made since 1989 from earlier US-made products, the Japanese serial numbering system should provide a clue. On Japanese models the serial number, unlike any of the US systems, usually has six digits plus a three-digit suffix (for example 901121-154).

IDENTIFICATION FEATURES	MODEL	MADE	PAGE
STYLE ONE (1939-58) Non-cutaway large body (approx 16in wide)			
USA			
One pickup, two controls	Electromatic Spanish 1st version	1939-42	86
One pickup, two controls, trapeze tailpiece	Electromatic Spanish 2nd version/ Corvette hollow body version	1949-56	86
One pickup, two controls, G-hole flat tailpiece	Clipper 1st version	1956-58	86
Two pickups, three controls	Electro II 1st version	1951-54	86
STYLE TWO (1951-81, 1989-current) One rounded cutaway on large body (approx 16in or approx 17in wide)			
USA: MODEL NAME OR LOGO ON GUITAR			
Anniversary on headstock, one pickup	Anniversary	1958-72	86
Anniversary on headstock, two close-spaced pickups	Anniversary Stereo	1961-63	87
Anniversary on headstock, two pickups	Anniversary two-pickup 1st version	1958-72	86
Anniversary on pickguard, frame-type tailpiece	Anniversary two-pickup 3rd version	1974-77	87
Chet Atkins Country Gentleman on headstock	Chet Atkins Country Gentleman 1st version	1957-61	87
Chet Atkins logo on pickguard, orange	Chet Atkins Hollow Body 1st version	1955-61	87
Chet Atkins logo on pickguard, one pickup	Chet Atkins Tennessean 1st version	1958-61	87
Chet Atkins Tennessean on pickguard, two pickups, fake f-holes	Chet Atkins Tennessean 2nd version	1961-72	87
Chet Atkins Tennessean on pickguard, two pickups, f-holes	Chet Atkins Tennessean 3rd version	1972-79	88
Country Club on nameplate over frame-type tailpiece	Country Club 4th version	1974-81	88
Electromatic on headstock, one or two pickups, trapeze tailpiece	Electromatic	1951-54	89
Electromatic on headstock, one pickup, G-hole flat tailpiece	Streamliner 1st version	1954-58	89
Falcon logo on pickguard, hump-top block or half-moon markers	White Falcon 1st version	1955-62	90
Falcon logo on pickguard, block markers	White Falcon 4th version	1974-78	90
Falcon logo on pickguard, two close-spaced pickups	White Falcon Stereo 1st version	1958-59	90
Falcon logo on pickguard, two controls & five selectors	White Falcon Stereo 2nd version	1959-62	90
Falcon logo on pickguard, two controls & five selectors, block markers	White Falcon Stereo 5th version	1974-78	90
Synchromatic on headstock, two pickups	Electro II 2nd version	1951-54	89
Van Eps on asymmetric headstock, seven strings	Van Eps seven-string 1st version	1968-72	89
Van Eps on asymmetric headstock, six strings	Van Eps six-string	1968-72	90
White Falcon on headstock	White Falcon 1st version	1958-62	90
USA: NO MODEL NAME OR LOGO ON GUITAR			
One pickup, bound fingerboard	Streamliner 1st version	1954-59	89
One single-coil pickup, dot markers	Clipper 2nd version	1957-72	88
One pickup attached to elongated pickguard	Convertible	1955-59	88
One pickup, elongated pickguard with or without controls	Sal Salvador	1959-66	89
Two close-spaced pickups	Country Club Stereo 1st version	1958-60	88
Two single-coil pickups, 'cat's-eye' soundholes	'Cat's-Eye Custom'	1964-67	87
Two single-coil pickups, trapeze tailpiece	Clipper 3rd version	1972-74	88
Two single-coil pickups, G-hole flat tailpiece	Anniversary two-pickup 2nd version	1972-74	87
Two single-coil pickups, G-hole flat tailpiece, gold-plated hardware	Country Club 1st version	1954-58	88
Two humbucker pickups, G-hole flat tailpiece, gold-plated hardware	Country Club 2nd version	1958-72	88
Two humbucker pickups, G-hole flat tailpiece, gold-plated hardware, truss-rod adjuster at neck heel	Country Club 3rd version	1972-74	88
Two humbucker pickups, asymmetric headstock, seven strings	Van Eps seven-string 2nd version	1972-78	90
Two humbucker pickups, two controls & five selectors	Country Club Stereo 2nd version	1960-65	89
Based on 1955-period original, but ebony fingerboard	Country Club 1955 Custom	1995-current	88
Based on 1955-period Hollow Body, but ebony fingerboard	Nashville 1955 Custom	1995-current	89

78

BODY STYLES
Each main model entry above includes a 'Style bar' to identify which of Gretsch's 20 distinctive body Styles is used. The styles are shown in silhouette, on the right, numbered 1 to 20.

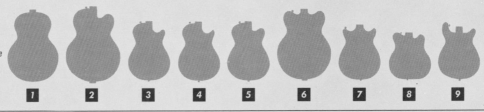

Based on 1955-period White Falcon, but 22 frets	White Falcon I — 1955 Custom	1995-current	90

JAPAN: MODEL NAME OR LOGO ON GUITAR

Anniversary on headstock, one pickup	Anniversary one-pickup	1993-current	90
Anniversary on headstock, two pickups	Anniversary two-pickup	1993-current	91
Brian Setzer signature on pickguard	Nashville Brian Setzer	1993-current	91
Country Classic I on headstock & pickguard	Country Classic I	1989-current	91
Falcon logo on pickguard, 22 frets, G-logo frame-type tailpiece, black	Black Falcon 6136BK	1992-current	91
Falcon logo on pickguard, 22 frets, G-logo frame-type tailpiece, black, chrome-plated hardware	Silver Falcon 6136SL	1995-current	91
Falcon logo on pickguard, 22 frets, G-logo frame-type tailpiece, white	White Falcon 6136	1990-current	92
Falcon logo on pickguard, 22 frets, vibrato tailpiece, black	Black Falcon 7593BK	1992-current	91
Falcon logo on pickguard, 22 frets, vibrato tailpiece, white	White Falcon 7593	1990-current	92
Synchromatic on headstock, vibrato tailpiece	Synchromatic 400MCV	1992-current	91
Synchromatic on headstock, harp-frame tailpiece	Synchromatic 6040MC	1994-current	92
Tennessee Rose on pickguard, f-holes	Tennessee Rose 6119	1989-current	92
Tennessee Rose on pickguard, fake f-holes, zero fret	Tennessee Rose 6119-1962	1993-current	92

JAPAN: NO MODEL NAME OR LOGO ON GUITAR

Horseshoe on headstock, block markers	Nashville 6120	1989-current	91
Horseshoe on headstock, half-moon markers, zero fret	Nashville 6120-1960	1992-current	91
Horseshoe on headstock, block markers, G-logo on body front	Nashville Western 6120W	1989-current	91
Steer head on headstock, triangular soundhole, one pickup	Rancher 6022CV	1992-current	91

STYLE THREE (1953-79,1989-current) One semi-pointed cutaway on small body (approx 13in wide)

USA: MODEL NAME OR LOGO ON GUITAR

Chet Atkins logo on pickguard	Chet Atkins Solid Body 1st version	1955-61	92
Penguin logo on pickguard	White Penguin 1st version	1955-61	93
Roc Jet on headstock	Roc Jet 1st version	1969-72	93

USA: NO MODEL NAME OR LOGO ON GUITAR

Black body front	Duo Jet 1st version	1953-61	92
Dark red, all controls on elliptical plate	Roc II	1973-75	93
Orange body front, four controls & one selector, steer head on pickguard	Round Up	1954-59	93
Orange body front, five controls & one selector, G-brand on body front	Country Roc	1974-79	92
Red body front	Jet Fire Bird 1st version	1955-61	92
Silver sparkle body front	Silver Jet 1st version	1954-61	93
Various color body fronts, truss-rod adjuster at neck heel, chrome-plated hardware	Roc Jet 2nd version	1972-79	93

JAPAN

Black body front, two humbucker pickups	Duo Jet 6128	1989-current	93
Black body front, two single-coil pickups	Duo Jet 6128-1957	1994-current	93
Blue pearl body front, two humbucker pickups	Sparkle Jet 6129T	1995-current	94
Blue pearl body front, two single-coil pickups	Sparkle Jet 6129-1957	1995-current	94
Orange body front, two humbucker pickups, G-logo on body front	Round Up	1989-current	93
Red body front, two humbucker pickups	Jet Firebird	1989-current	93
Silver sparkle body front, two humbucker pickups	Silver Jet 6129	1989-current	93
Silver sparkle body front, two single-coil pickups	Silver Jet 6129-1957	1994-current	94
Various color sparkle body fronts (not silver), two humbucker pickups	Sparkle Jet 6129	1995-current	94
Various color sparkle body fronts (not silver), two single-coil pickups	Sparkle Jet 6129-1957	1995-current	94
White, two single-coil pickups, penguin logo on pickguard	White Penguin	1993-94	94

STYLE FOUR (1957-60) One sharp-pointed cutaway on small body (approx 13in wide)

USA

Two large f-holes on small body	Rambler 1st version	1957-60	94

10 **11** **12** **13** **14** **15** **16** **17** **18** **19** **20**

STYLE FIVE (1960-62) One rounded cutaway on small body (approx 13in wide)

USA

Two large f-holes on small body	Rambler 2nd version	1960-62	94

STYLE SIX (1961-81, 1989-current) Twin shallow cutaways on large body (approx 16in or approx 17in wide)

USA: MODEL NAME OR LOGO ON GUITAR

Black Hawk on headstock	Black Hawk	1967-70	94
Chet Atkins Country Gentleman on headstock, fake f-holes	Chet Atkins Country Gentleman 2nd version	1961-67	94
Chet Atkins Country Gentleman on headstock & pickguard, fake f-holes	Chet Atkins Country Gentleman 2nd version	1967-72	94
Chet Atkins Country Gentleman on pickguard, f-holes	Chet Atkins Country Gentleman 3rd version	1972-81	95
Chet Atkins logo on pickguard, fake f-holes, orange	Chet Atkins Hollow Body 2nd version	1961-67	95
Chet Atkins Nashville on headstock & pickguard, fake f-holes	Chet Atkins Nashville 1st version	1967-72	95
Chet Atkins Nashville on pickguard only, f-holes	Chet Atkins Nashville 2nd version	1972-79	95
Falcon logo on pickguard, truss-rod adjuster at neck heel	White Falcon 3rd version	1972-80	96
Falcon logo on pickguard, truss-rod adjuster at neck heel, two controls & five or six selectors	White Falcon Stereo 4th version	1972-81	97
Monkees on truss-rod cover & pickguard	Monkees	1966-67	95
Ronny Lee on headstock, fake f-holes	Ronny Lee	1962-63	95
Sam Goody on headstock, G-shape soundholes	Sam Goody	1967	96
Streamliner on headstock	Streamliner 2nd version	1968-72	96
Viking on headstock & pickguard	Viking 1st version	1964-72	96
Viking on pickguard only, truss-rod adjuster at neck heel	Viking 2nd version	1972-74	96
White Falcon on headstock, falcon logo on pickguard	White Falcon 2nd version	1962-72	96
White Falcon on headstock, falcon logo on pickguard, two controls & five or six selectors	White Falcon Stereo 3rd version	1962-72	96

USA: NO MODEL NAME OR LOGO ON GUITAR

Dot markers, three controls & two selectors	Broadkaster semi-hollow body 1st version	1975-77	94
Dot markers, five controls & one selector	Broadkaster semi-hollow body 2nd version	1977-79	94
Half-moon markers, truss-rod adjuster at neck heel, G-hole flat tailpiece	Streamliner 3rd version	1972-75	96
Half-moon/dot markers, diagonal stripes on truss-rod cover & pickguard	Rally	1967-68	95
Triangle markers, 12-string headstock	12-string	1966-70	97

JAPAN: MODEL NAME OR LOGO ON GUITAR

Country Classic II on headstock & pickguard, f-holes	Country Classic II 6122	1989-current	97
Country Classic II on headstock & pickguard, fake f-holes, zero fret	Country Classic II 6122-1962	1993-current	97
Falcon logo on pickguard, 22 frets, black	Black Falcon 7594BK	1992-current	97
Falcon logo on pickguard, 22 frets, black, chrome-plated hardware	Silver Falcon 7594SL	1995-current	97
Falcon logo on pickguard; 22 frets, white	White Falcon 7594	1990-current	97

STYLE SEVEN (1961-69) Twin semi-pointed cutaways on small body (approx 13in wide)

USA

Black body front	Duo Jet 2nd version	1961-69	98
Orange body front, Chet Atkins logo on pickguard	Chet Atkins Solid Body 2nd version	1961-62	97
Red body front	Jet Fire Bird 2nd version	1961-69	98
Silver sparkle body front	Silver Jet 2nd version	1961-63	98
Various color sparkle body fronts	Duo Jet 2nd version	1963-69	98
White	White Penguin 2nd version	1961-62	98

STYLE EIGHT (1961) Slightly-offset rounded cutaways on small body (approx 13in wide)

USA

Solid body with detachable slide-on hinged back section	Bikini	1961	98

STYLE NINE (1961-62) Two rounded cutaways (with longer left horn) on small body (approx 13in wide)

USA

Slab body, one pickup at bridge	Corvette solidbody 1st version	1961-62	98

BODY STYLES

Each main model entry above includes a 'Style bar' to identify which of Gretsch's 20 distinctive body Styles is used. The styles are shown in silhouette, on the right, numbered 1 to 20.

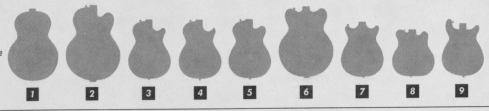

STYLE TEN (1962-65) Two pointed cutaways (with long left horn) on small body (approx 13in wide)

USA

Beveled-edge body, one pickup	Corvette solidbody 2nd version one-pickup	1962-65	98
Beveled-edge body, one pickup, pad on body back	Princess	1962-63	99
Beveled-edge body, one pickup, red/white striped pickguard	Twist	1962-63	99
Beveled-edge body, two pickups	Corvette solidbody 2nd version two-pickup	1963-65	99

STYLE ELEVEN (1965-70) Two pointed cutaways (with long left horn) on small body (approx 13in wide) with cut-out in base

USA

Two- & four-tuners-per-side-headstock, one pickup	Corvette solidbody 3rd version one-pickup	1965-70	99
Two- & four-tuners-per-side-headstock, two pickups	Corvette solidbody 3rd version two-pickup	1965-70	99

STYLE TWELVE (1963-66) Offset pointed cutaways on asymmetrically curved large body (approx 16in wide)

USA

Model name on red/black body, two-/four-tuners-per-side-headstock	Astro-Jet	1963-66	99

STYLE THIRTEEN (1972-79) One rounded cutaway (& angled-in left upper bout) on large body (approx 17in wide)

USA

Chet Atkins on pickguard, controls on body	Deluxe Chet	1972-73	99
Super Chet on pickguard with controls along edge	Super Chet	1972-79	99

STYLE FOURTEEN (1975-76) Offset rounded cutaways on small body (approx 13in wide)

USA

Two pickups, all controls and jack on pickguard	Broadkaster solidbody version	1975-76	100

STYLE FIFTEEN (1977-81) Twin rounded cutaways on small body (approx 12in wide)

USA

22-fret lamtnated through-neck	Committee	1977-81	100

STYLE SIXTEEN (1977-81) Offset pointed cutaways on small body (approx 12in wide) with curved cut-out in base

USA

Six-tuners-in-line headstock	TK 300	1977-81	100

STYLE SEVENTEEN (1977-80) One sharp-pointed cutaway (& angled-in left upper bout) on large body (approx 16in wide)

USA

Small block markers, controls on body	Atkins Axe	1977-80	100
Small block markers, controls on elliptical plate	Super Axe	1977-80	100

JAPAN

Small block markers, controls on body, truss-rod adjuster at headstock	Axe	1995-current	100

STYLE EIGHTEEN (1979-81) One pointed cutaway (& angled-in left upper bout) on small body (approx 13in wide)

USA

24-fret bolt-on neck, one pickup	Beast BST-1000/1500 one-pickup	1979-81	100
24-fret bolt-on neck, two pickups	Beast BST-1000 two-pickup	1979-81	101

STYLE NINETEEN (1979-80) Twin pointed cutaways on small body (approx 13in wide)

USA

22-fret bolt-on neck	Beast BST-2000	1979-80	101

STYLE TWENTY (1979-81) Offset pointed cutaways on small body (approx 13in wide)

USA

24-fret laminated through-neck on carved-edge body	Beast BST-5000	1979-81	101

10   11   12   13   14   15   16   17   18   19   20

Unlike some brands, Gretsch allotted names to virtually all its models, and many instruments carry their title on headstock and/or pickguard. This provides easy recognition – but please note that the company sometimes used the same model name for radically different instruments.

Another useful ID clue is provided by the four-digit model number (not to be confused with the serial number) allocated to most models, and this can usually be found on a label posted somewhere within the instrument. For Gretsch, differences in construction, components and (especially) cosmetics warranted a different numerical designation, so the code can be a helpful pointer to identity. However, there has been considerable repetition and duplication of numbers, and this can cause confusion, so further indicators should be used to confirm the actual model.

MODEL NO.	MODEL NAME	PAGE	MODEL NO.	MODEL NAME	PAGE
USA			**USA**		
6023	Bikini	98	6129	Silver Jet	93, 98
6075	12-string	97	6130	Roc Jet	93
6076	12-string	97	6130	Round Up	93
6079	Van Eps	89	6131	Jet Fire Bird	92, 98
6080	Van Eps	89	6132	Corvette	98
6081	Van Eps	90	6133	Corvette	98
6082	Van Eps	90	6134	Corvette	98
6100	Black Hawk	94	6134	White Penguin	93, 98
6101	Black Hawk	94	6135	Corvette	99
6101	Country Club Stereo	88	6136	White Falcon	90, 96
6102	Country Club Stereo	88	6136	White Falcon I-1955 Custom	90
6102	Streamliner	96	6137	White Falcon Stereo	90, 96
6103	Country Club Stereo	88	6182	Corvette	86
6103	Streamliner	96	6182	Electromatic Spanish	86
6104	Rally	95	6183	Corvette	86
6105	Rally	95	6183	Electromatic Spanish	86
6106	Princess	99	6184	Corvette	86
6109	Twist	99	6185	Electromatic Spanish	86
6110	Twist (vibrato)	99	6186	Clipper	86
6111	Anniversary Stereo	87	6187	Clipper	86
6112	Anniversary Stereo	87	6187	Electro II	86
6115	Rambler	94	6187	Viking	96
6117	'Cat's Eye Custom'	87	6188	Clipper	86
6117	Anniversary two-pickup	86	6188	Electro II	86
6118	Anniversary two-pickup	86	6188	Viking	96
6119	Chet Atkins Tennessean	87	6189	Electromatic	89
6120	Chet Atkins Hollow Body	87, 95	6189	Streamliner	89
6120	Chet Atkins Nashville	95	6189	Viking	96
6120	Nashville 1955 Custom	89	6190	Electromatic	89
6121	Chet Atkins Solid Body	92	6190	Streamliner	89
6122	Chet Atkins Country Gentleman	87, 94	6191	Electromatic	89
6123	Monkees	95	6191	Streamliner	89
6124	Anniversary	90	6192	Country Club	88
6125	Anniversary	90	6192	Electro II	89
6126	Astro-Jet	99	6193	Country Club	88
6127	Roc Jet	93	6193	Electro II	89
6128	Duo Jet	92, 98	6196	Country Club	88

MODEL NO.	MODEL NAME	PAGE
USA		
6199	Convertible	88
6199	Sal Salvador	89
7555	Clipper	88
7560	Anniversary	87
7565	Streamliner	96
7566	Streamliner	96
7575	Country Club	88
7576	Country Club	88
7577	Country Club	88
7580	Van Eps	90
7581	Van Eps	90
7585	Viking	96
7586	Viking	96
7593	White Falcon	90
7593	White Falcon Stereo	90
7594	White Falcon	96
7595	White Falcon Stereo	97
7600	Broadkaster	100
7601	Broadkaster	100
7603	Broadkaster	94
7604	Broadkaster	94
7607	Broadkaster	94
7608	Broadkaster	94
7609	Broadkaster	94
7610	Roc Jet	93
7611	Roc Jet	93
7612	Roc Jet	93
7613	Roc Jet	93
7620	Country Roc	92
7621	Roc II	93
7624	TK 300	100
7625	TK 300	100
7628	Committee	100
7655	Chet Atkins Tennessean	88
7660	Chet Atkins Nashville	95
7670	Chet Atkins Country Gentleman	95
7676	Country Squire	95
7680	Deluxe Chet	99
7680	Super Axe	100
7681	Deluxe Chet	99
7681	Super Axe	100
7682	Super Axe	100
7685	Atkins Axe	100
7686	Atkins Axe	100
7690	Super Chet	99
7691	Super Chet	99
8210	Beast BST-1000	100
8211	Beast BST-1000	101
8215	Beast BST-1000	101
8216	Beast BST-1000	100
8217	Beast BST-1500	100
8220	Beast BST-2000	101
8221	Beast BST-2000	101
8250	Beast BST-5000	101

MODEL NO.	MODEL NAME	PAGE
JAPAN		

The more recent Japanese-made Gretsch electrics adopt a similar system of model numbers, and even employ some of the original numbers for the revived models or near-equivalents of old models. In addition, various suffixes are used to denote variations in construction, components and/or cosmetics.

MODEL NO.	MODEL NAME	PAGE
400CV	Synchromatic 400CV	91
400MCV	Synchromatic 400MCV	91
6022CV	Rancher 6022CV	91
6040MC-SS	Synchromatic 6040MC-SS	92
6117	Anniversary	91
6118	Anniversary	91
6119	Tennessee Rose 6119	92
6119-1962	Tennessee Rose 6119-1962	92
6120	Nashville 6120	91
6120BS	Nashville 6120	91
6120GR	Nashville 6120	91
6120SSL	Nashville Brian Setzer	91
6120SSU	Nashville Brian Setzer	91
6120SSUGR	Nashville Brian Setzer	91
6120TM	Nashville	91
6120W	Nashville Western 6120W	91
6120-1960	Nashville 6120-1960	91
6121	Round Up	93
6122	Country Classic II 6122	97
6122-S	Country Classic I	91
6122-1962	Country Classic II 6122-1962	90
6124	Anniversary	90
6125	Anniversary	90
6128	Duo Jet 6128	93
6128-1957	Duo Jet 6128-1957	93
6129	Silver Jet 6129	93
6129	Sparkle Jet 6129	94
6129-1957	Silver Jet 6129-1957	94
6129-1957	Sparkle Jet 6129-1957	94
6131	Jet Firebird	93
6134	White Penguin	94
6136	White Falcon 6136	92
6136BK	Black Falcon 6136BK	91
6136SL	Silver Falcon 6136SL	91
7593	White Falcon 7593	92
7593BK	Black Falcon 7593BK	91
7594	White Falcon 7594	97
7594BK	Black Falcon 7594BK	97
7594SL	Silver Falcon 7594SL	97
7685	Axe	100

83

REFERENCE LISTING

The main Reference Listing (pages 86-101) uses a simple condensed format to convey a large amount of information about every Gretsch electric model, and the following notes are intended to ensure that you gain the most from this unique inventory.

The list covers all electric Spanish guitars issued by Gretsch between 1939 and 1995. Each is allocated to one of 20 distinctive body shapes, called STYLES, which are numbered in chronological order of introduction. Corresponding body silhouettes are ranged along the bottom of each pair of pages; those shown in a darker shade relate to the accompanying text. Under each style heading the relevant models are listed in alphabetical sequence, and the model numbers employed by Gretsch to denote differences are also included in the listings.

At the head of each entry is the model name (and number if applicable) in **bold type**, followed by a date or range of dates showing the production period of the instrument. These dates and any others in the Reference Section are naturally as accurate as possible, but should still be considered approximate. As with any other guitar company, there is *no* guaranteed foolproof method to pinpoint exact periods of Gretsch manufacture, so all dating should be considered as a guide, not as gospel. Note that 'c' in front of a date stands for 'circa', meaning 'about'.

In *italics*, following the model name/number and production dates, is a brief, one-sentence identification of the guitar in question. Just as in the preceding Model Identification Index (pages 78-81), this is intended to help you recognize a specific model at a glance. To do this we have noted the more obvious features that in combination are unique to that model.

For some guitars, usually those that exist in different versions, there may be a sentence below this, reading 'Similar to ... except'. This will refer to another model entry, and the accompanying description will list any major differences between the two.

In most entries there will be a list of specification points, separated into groups, providing details of the model's main features. In the order listed the points refer to:

▌ Neck, fingerboard; position markers; frets; location of truss-rod adjuster; headstock.
▌ Body; finish.
▌ Pickups.
▌ Controls.
▌ Pickguard.
▌ Bridge, tailpiece.
▌ Hardware plating finish.
▌ Special features, if any.

Note that some Special Order options were and are available on various models, but not all are recorded in the Reference Listing.

Of course, not every model will need all eight points, and to avoid undue repetition we have considered a number of features to be common to all Gretsch guitars. They are:

Glued-in neck unless stated.

Headstock with three tuners each side unless stated.

All controls on body front unless stated.

Side-mounted jack unless stated.

Metal bridge saddle(s) with wooden or metal base unless stated.

Nickel- or chrome-plated hardware unless stated.

Some models were made in a number of variations, and where applicable these are listed, in *italics*, after the specification points. Any other general comments are also made here, in similar fashion.

Some entries comprise only a short listing. This is usually because the model concerned is a reissue of, or a re-creation based on, an earlier guitar, and the text will usually refer the reader to the original instrument. Alternative name/number designations are also listed as separate, brief entries. Reading 'See...', each will refer to the appropriate main model(s).

All this information is designed to tell you more about your Gretsch guitar. By using the general history and illustrations earlier in this book, combined with the knowledge obtained from the Reference Section, you should be able to build up a very full picture of your instrument and its pedigree.

GRETSCH REFERENCE LISTING:
ALL ELECTRIC MODELS 1939-1995

STYLE ONE (1939-58) USA

Non-cutaway large body

CLIPPER first version 1956-58 *One pickup, two controls, G-hole flat tailpiece.*
■ Unbound rosewood fingerboard, dot markers; 21 frets; truss-rod adjuster at headstock.
■ Hollow archtop bound body with two large f-holes; sunburst (6186), beige/gray (6187) or natural (6188).
■ One single-coil pickup at neck.
■ Two controls (volume, tone).
■ Colored plastic pickguard.
■ Single-saddle wooden bridge, separate G-hole flat tailpiece.
Some examples in cream/gray (6187). Succeeded by one-cutaway second version, see listing under STYLE TWO.

CORVETTE hollow body version 1954-56
One pickup, two controls, trapeze tailpiece.
■ Unbound rosewood fingerboard, dot markers; 20 frets; Electromatic on headstock.
■ Hollow archtop bound body with two large f-holes; sunburst (6182) or natural (6183) (or gold 6184 from c1955).
■ One single-coil pickup at neck.
■ Two controls (volume, tone).
■ Tortoiseshell or colored plastic pickguard.
■ Single-saddle wooden bridge, separate trapeze tailpiece.
Some examples with 21 frets.
Previously known as ELECTROMATIC SPANISH second version, see right.

ELECTRO II first version 1951-54 *Two pickups, three controls, 20 frets.*
■ Bound rosewood fingerboard, block markers; 20 frets; Electromatic on headstock.
■ Hollow archtop bound body with two large f-holes; sunburst (6187) or natural (6188).
■ Two single-coil pickups.
■ Three controls (two volume, one tone).
■ Single-saddle wooden bridge, separate trapeze tailpiece.
Also one-cutaway version, see listing under STYLE TWO

ELECTROMATIC SPANISH first version 1939-42 *One pickup, two controls.*
■ Hollow archtop body with two f-holes; sunburst.
■ One single-coil pickup.
■ Two controls (volume, tone).
No other information available.

ELECTROMATIC SPANISH second version 1949-54 *One pickup, two controls, trapeze tailpiece.*
■ Unbound rosewood fingerboard, dot markers; 20 frets; Electromatic on headstock.
■ Hollow archtop bound body with two large f-holes; sunburst (6185; 6182 from c1952), or natural (6185N c1951-52; 6183 from c1952).
■ One single-coil pickup at neck.
■ Two controls (volume, tone).
■ Tortoiseshell plastic pickguard.
■ Single-saddle wooden bridge, separate trapeze tailpiece.
Known as CORVETTE hollow body version from c1954, see separate listing.

STYLE TWO (1951-81, 1995-current) USA

One rounded cutaway on large body

ANNIVERSARY one-pickup 1958-72
Anniversary on headstock, one pickup at neck.
■ Unbound ebony fingerboard (rosewood from c1960), half-moon markers; 21 frets; truss-rod adjuster at headstock; model nameplate on headstock.
■ Hollow archtop bound body with two large f-holes; sunburst (6124) or light/dark green (6125).
■ One humbucker pickup at neck (one single-coil pickup from c1960).
■ One control (volume) and one selector.
■ Colored plastic pickguard.
■ Six-saddle bridge, separate G-hole flat tailpiece.
■ Clip-on vibrato lever c1962-65.
Some examples with 22 frets.
Some examples in light/dark brown (6125) from c1963.

ANNIVERSARY two-pickup first version 1958-72 *Anniversary on headstock, two pickups.*
■ Unbound (bound from c1962) ebony fingerboard (rosewood from c1960), half-moon markers; 21 frets (plus zero fret from c1968); truss-rod adjuster at headstock; model nameplate on headstock.
■ Hollow archtop bound body with two large f-holes; sunburst (6117) or light/dark green (6118).

BODY STYLES
Each main model entry above includes a 'Style bar' to identify which of Gretsch's 20 distinctive body Styles is used. The styles are shown in silhouette, on the right, numbered 1 to 20.

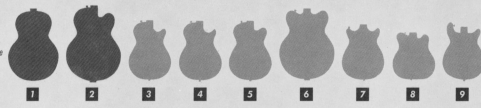

1 2 3 4 5 6 7 8 9

■ Two humbucker pickups (two single-coil pickups from c1960).
■ Three controls (all volume) and two selectors.
■ Colored plastic pickguard with Gretsch logo.
■ Six-saddle bridge, separate G-hole flat tailpiece.
■ Clip-on vibrato lever c1962-65.
Some examples with 20 or 22 frets.
Some examples in light/dark brown (6118) from c1963.
Also known as DOUBLE ANNIVERSARY.

ANNIVERSARY two-pickup second version

1972-74 Two single-coil pickups, G-hole flat tailpiece.
Similar to first version, except:
■ 22 frets and zero fret; truss-rod adjuster at neck heel; no model nameplate on headstock.
■ Hollow archtop bound body with two f-holes; sunburst (7560).

ANNIVERSARY two-pickup third version

1974-77 Anniversary on pickguard, frame-type tailpiece.
Similar to second version, except:
■ Block markers.
■ Three controls (two volume, one tone) and one selector.
■ Colored plastic pickguard with Anniversary logo.
■ Six-saddle bridge, separate frame-type tailpiece.

ANNIVERSARY STEREO

1961-63 Model name on headstock, two close-spaced split-polepiece single-coil pickups.
Similar to ANNIVERSARY two-pickup first version, except:
■ Sunburst (6111) or light/dark green (6112).
■ Two split-polepiece single-coil pickups (close-spaced – one at neck, one in central position).
■ Two controls (both volume) and three selectors.

'CAT'S-EYE CUSTOM'

1964-67 'Cat's-Eye' soundholes.
■ Bound rosewood fingerboard, half-moon markers; 22 frets plus zero fret; truss-rod adjuster at headstock.
■ Hollow archtop bound body with two 'cat's eye' soundholes; various colors (6117).
■ Two single-coil pickups.
■ Four controls (two volume, two tone) and one selector.
■ Colored plastic pickguard.
■ Six-saddle bridge, separate G-hole flat tailpiece.
Some examples with 21 frets.

CHET ATKINS COUNTRY GENTLEMAN first version

1957-61 Chet Atkins Country Gentleman on headstock.
■ Bound ebony fingerboard, half-moon markers; 22 frets (plus zero fret from c1959); truss-rod adjuster at headstock; model nameplate on headstock.
■ Hollow archtop bound body with two fake f-holes; dark brown (6122).
■ Two humbucker pickups.
■ Three controls (all volume) and two selectors.
■ Colored plastic pickguard.
■ Single-saddle bridge, separate vibrato tailpiece.
■ Gold-plated hardware.
Some examples with f-holes.
Some examples with Chet Atkins logo on pickguard.
Succeeded by twin-cutaway second version, see listing under STYLE SIX.

CHET ATKINS HOLLOW BODY first version

1955-61 Chet Atkins logo on pickguard, orange.
■ Bound rosewood fingerboard (ebony from c1958), engraved block markers (plain block from c1956; hump-top block from c1957; half-moon from c1958); 22 frets (plus zero fret from c1959); truss-rod adjuster at headstock; steer head on headstock (horseshoe from c1956).

■ Hollow archtop bound body with two large f-holes and G-brand on front (no G-brand from c1957); orange (6120).
■ Two single-coil pickups (two humbucker pickups from c1958).
■ Four controls (three volume, one tone) and one selector (three controls – all volume – and two selectors from c1958).
■ Colored plastic pickguard with Chet Atkins logo.
■ Single-saddle bridge, separate vibrato tailpiece.
■ Gold-plated hardware.
Some examples with 21 frets.
Some examples in red (6120).
Succeeded by twin-cutaway second version, see listing under STYLE SIX.

CHET ATKINS TENNESSEAN first version

1958-61 Chet Atkins logo on pickguard, one humbucker pickup near bridge.
■ Unbound ebony fingerboard, half-moon markers; 22 frets (plus zero fret from c1959); truss-rod adjuster at headstock.
■ Hollow archtop bound body with two large f-holes; dark red (6119).
■ One humbucker pickup near bridge.
■ One control (volume) and one selector.
■ Colored plastic pickguard with Chet Atkins logo.
■ Single-saddle bridge, separate vibrato tailpiece.
Some examples with 21 frets.

CHET ATKINS TENNESSEAN second version

1961-72 Chet Atkins Tennessean on pickguard, two single-coil pickups, fake f-holes.
Similar to first version, except:
■ Bound rosewood fingerboard; model nameplate on headstock (c1967-71).
■ Hollow archtop bound body with two fake f-holes; dark red or dark brown (6119).
■ Two single-coil pickups.
■ Three controls (all volume) and three selectors.

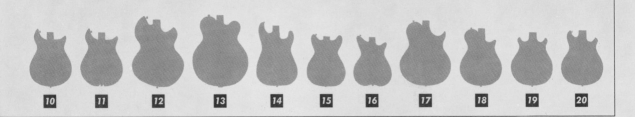

10 11 12 13 14 15 16 17 18 19 20

■ Colored plastic pickguard with model name.

CHET ATKINS TENNESSEAN third version 1972-79 Model name on pickguard, two single-coil pickups, f-holes.
Similar to second version, except:
■ Truss-rod adjuster at neck heel; no model nameplate on headstock.
■ Hollow archtop bound body with two f-holes; dark red (7655).
■ Three controls (all volume) and two selectors from c1978.
■ Six-saddle bridge.

CLIPPER second version 1957-72 One single-coil pickup at neck, dot markers.
■ Unbound rosewood fingerboard, dot markers; 21 frets; truss-rod adjuster on headstock.
■ Hollow archtop bound body with two large f-holes; sunburst (6186), or natural (6187) c1958-59.
■ One single-coil pickup at neck.
■ Two controls (volume, tone) (located near body edge from c1967).
■ Colored plastic pickguard.
■ Single-saddle wooden bridge, separate trapeze tailpiece or G-hole flat tailpiece.
Some examples with 22 frets, in cream/gray (6187).
Succeeded non-cutaway first version, see listing under STYLE ONE.

CLIPPER third version 1972-75 Two single-coil pickups, trapeze tailpiece.
■ Bound rosewood fingerboard, half-moon markers; 22 frets plus zero fret; truss-rod adjuster at neck heel.
■ Hollow archtop bound body with two f-holes; sunburst/black (7555).
■ Two single-coil pickups.
■ Three controls (all volume) and two selectors.
■ Colored plastic pickguard.
■ Six-saddle bridge, separate trapeze tailpiece.

CONVERTIBLE 1955-59 One pickup attached to elongated pickguard.
■ Bound rosewood fingerboard (ebony from c1958), hump-top block markers (half-moon from c1958); 21 frets; truss-rod adjuster at headstock.
■ Hollow archtop bound body with two large f-holes; cream/brown (6199).
■ One single-coil pickup, attached to pickguard.
■ Two controls (volume, tone) mounted on pickguard.
■ Colored elongated plastic pickguard.
■ Single-saddle wooden bridge, separate G-hole flat tailpiece.
■ Gold-plated hardware.
Some examples in sunburst.
Some examples in yellow/brown (6199) from c1958.
Known as SAL SALVADOR from c1959, see separate listing.

COUNTRY CLUB first version 1954-58 Two single-coil pickups, G-hole flat tailpiece, gold-plated hardware.
■ Bound rosewood fingerboard, block markers (hump-top block from c1955); 21 frets; truss-rod adjuster at headstock.
■ Hollow archtop bound body with two large f-holes; sunburst (6192), natural (6193) or green (6196).
■ Two single-coil pickups.
■ Four controls (three volume, one tone) and one selector.
■ Tortoiseshell plastic pickguard (colored plastic from c1955).
■ Six-saddle bridge, separate G-hole flat tailpiece.
■ Gold-plated hardware.
Some examples in light/dark gray (6196) and other colors.
Previously known as ELECTRO II second version, see separate listing.

COUNTRY CLUB second version 1958-72 Two humbucker pickups, G-hole flat tailpiece, gold-plated hardware.
Similar to first version, except:

■ Bound ebony fingerboard, half-moon markers; 21 frets (plus zero fret from c1959).
■ Two humbucker pickups.
■ Three controls (all volume) and two selectors (three selectors from c1962; +1 string damper control c1962-64).
■ Pad on body back c1962-63.
■ String damper and control c1962-64.
Stereo pickups and circuitry option c1958, see COUNTRY CLUB STEREO first version.

COUNTRY CLUB third version 1972-74 Two humbucker pickups, G-hole flat tailpiece, gold-plated hardware, truss-rod adjuster at neck heel.
Similar to second version, except:
■ Truss-rod adjuster at neck heel.
■ Hollow archtop bound body, two f-holes; sunburst (7575) or natural (7576).

COUNTRY CLUB fourth version 1974-81 Country Club on nameplate over frame-type tailpiece.
Similar to third version, except:
■ Block markers; 22 frets.
■ Natural (7576), brown (7577) c1977.
■ Five controls (three volume, two tone) and one selector.
■ Separate frame-type tailpiece with model nameplate overlay.

COUNTRY CLUB 1955 CUSTOM 1995-current Re-issue based on 1955-period original, but with bound ebony fingerboard.

COUNTRY CLUB STEREO first version 1958-60 Two close-spaced humbucker pickups.
■ Bound ebony fingerboard, half-moon markers; 21 frets (plus zero fret from c1959); truss-rod adjuster at headstock.
■ Hollow archtop bound body with two large f-holes; sunburst (6101), natural (6102) or green (6103).
■ Two split-polepiece humbucker pickups (close-spaced – one at neck, one in central position).
■ Two controls and three selectors.

BODY STYLES
Each main model entry above includes a 'Style bar' to identify which of Gretsch's 20 distinctive body Styles is used. The styles are shown in silhouette, on the right, numbered 1 to 20.

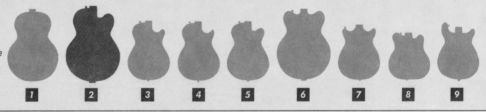

■ Colored plastic pickguard.
■ Six-saddle bridge, separate G-hole flat tailpiece.
■ Gold-plated hardware.
Some examples with non-split-polepiece humbucker pickups.
Some examples with model numbers as COUNTRY CLUB second version.

COUNTRY CLUB STEREO second version 1960-65 *Two humbucker pickups, two controls and five selectors.*
Similar to first version, except:
■ Two humbucker pickups.
■ Two controls (both volume) and five selectors (plus one string damper control c1962-64).
■ Pad on body back c1962-64.
■ String damper and control c1962-64.

COUNTRY GENTLEMAN See CHET ATKINS COUNTRY GENTLEMAN first version.

DOUBLE ANNIVERSARY See ANNIVERSARY two-pickup listings.

ELECTRO II second version 1951-54
Synchromatic on headstock, two single-coil pickups.
■ Bound rosewood fingerboard, block markers; 21 frets; truss-rod adjuster at body end of neck; Synchromatic on headstock.
■ Hollow archtop bound body; sunburst (6192) or natural (6193).
■ Two single-coil pickups.
■ Three controls (two volume, one tone) (four controls – two volume, two tone – from c1952; one selector from c1954).
■ Tortoiseshell plastic pickguard.
■ Single-saddle wooden bridge (six-saddle bridge from c1952), separate harp-frame or G-hole flat tailpiece.
■ Gold-plated hardware.
Some examples with 19 frets.
Also non-cutaway version, see listing under STYLE ONE.
Known as COUNTRY CLUB first version from c1954, see separate listing.

ELECTROMATIC 1951-54 *Electromatic on headstock, one or two single-coil pickups, trapeze tailpiece.*
■ Bound rosewood fingerboard, block markers; 21 frets; Electromatic on headstock.
■ Hollow archtop bound body with two large f-holes; sunburst (6190) or natural (6191).
■ One single-coil pickup at neck.
■ Two controls (volume, tone).
■ Tortoiseshell plastic pickguard.
■ Six-saddle bridge, separate trapeze tailpiece.
Some examples with two single-coil pickups (6189).
Known as STREAMLINER first version from c1954, see separate listing.

HOLLOW BODY See CHET ATKINS HOLLOW BODY first version listing.

NASHVILLE 1955 CUSTOM 1995-current *Reissue based on CHET ATKINS HOLLOW BODY (6120) 1955-period original, but with ebony fingerboard.*

PROJECT-O-SONIC See COUNTRY CLUB STEREO and WHITE FALCON STEREO listings.

SAL SALVADOR 1959-66 *One pickup, elongated pickguard with or without controls.*
■ Bound ebony fingerboard, half-moon markers (block from c1964); 21 frets (plus zero fret from c1960); truss-rod adjuster at headstock.
■ Hollow archtop bound body with two large f-holes; sunburst (6199).
■ One humbucker pickup (one single-coil from c1962) attached to pickguard (mounted on body from c1964).
■ Two controls (volume, tone) mounted on pickguard (mounted on body from c1964).
■ Colored elongated plastic pickguard.
■ Single-saddle wooden bridge, separate G-hole flat tailpiece.

■ Gold-plated hardware.
Previously known as CONVERTIBLE, see separate listing.

STREAMLINER first version 1954-59 *One pickup, bound fingerboard.*
■ Bound rosewood fingerboard, block markers (hump-top block from c1955); 21 frets; truss-rod adjuster at headstock; Electromatic on headstock until c1958.
■ Hollow archtop bound body with two large f-holes; gold (6189), yellow/brown (6189), sunburst (6190) or natural (6191).
■ One single-coil pickup at neck (one humbucker from c1958).
■ Two controls (volume, tone) (volume plus one selector from c1958).
■ Colored plastic pickguard.
■ Six-saddle bridge, separate G-hole flat tailpiece.
Previously known as ELECTROMATIC, see separate listing.
Also twin-cutaway version, see listing under STYLE SIX.

TENNESSEAN See CHET ATKINS TENNESSEAN listings.

VAN EPS seven-string first version 1968-72
Van Eps on asymmetric headstock, seven strings.
■ Bound ebony fingerboard, half-moon markers; 21 frets plus zero fret; truss-rod adjuster at headstock; model nameplate on headstock; four and three tuners-per-side headstock.
■ Hollow archtop bound body with two large f-holes; sunburst (6079) or brown (6080).
■ Two humbucker pickups.
■ Three controls (and three selectors.
■ Colored plastic pickguard.
■ Bar-frame 'Floating Sound' unit plus single-saddle wooden bridge, separate G-hole flat tailpiece.
■ Gold-plated hardware.

89

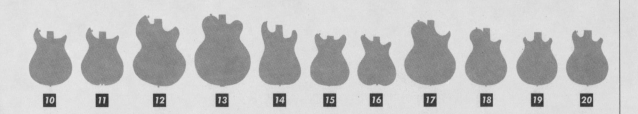

10   11   12   13   14   15   16   17   18   19   20

VAN EPS seven-string second version 1972-78 *Two humbucker pickups, asymmetric headstock, seven strings.*
Similar to first version, except:
▌ Truss-rod adjuster at neck heel; no model nameplate on headstock.
▌ Sunburst (7580), or brown (7581) c1972.
▌ Bar-frame 'Floating Sound' unit plus six-saddle bridge.
Some late examples with three controls (all volume) and two selectors; no 'Floating Sound' unit; single-saddle wooden bridge; chrome-plated hardware.

VAN EPS six-string 1968-72 *Van Eps on asymmetric headstock, six strings.*
Similar to VAN EPS seven-string first version, except:
▌ Three tuners-per-side asymmetric headstock.
▌ Sunburst (6081) or brown (6082).

WHITE FALCON first version 1955-62 *Falcon logo on pickguard, hump-top block or half-moon markers.*
▌ Bound ebony fingerboard, engraved hump-top block markers (half-moon from c1958); 21 frets (plus zero fret from c1959); truss-rod adjuster at headstock; vertical Gretsch logo on headstock (horizontal type plus model nameplate from c1958).
▌ Hollow archtop bound body with two large f-holes; white (6136).
▌ Two single-coil pickups (two humbucker pickups from c1958).
▌ Four controls (three volume, one tone) and one selector (three controls – all volume – and two selectors c1958-61; three controls – all volume – and three selectors, plus two string damper controls from c1961.
▌ Colored plastic pickguard with falcon logo.
▌ Six-saddle bridge, separate G-logo tubular frame-type tailpiece.
▌ Gold-plated hardware.

▌ Pad on body back from c1961.
▌ Double string damper and two controls from c1961.
Some examples with 22 frets.
Some examples with horizontal Gretsch logo without model nameplate.
Some examples in black.
Some examples with optional separate vibrato tailpiece.
Succeeded by twin-cutaway second version, see listing under STYLE SIX.

WHITE FALCON fourth version 1974-78 *Falcon logo on pickguard, block markers.*
▌ Bound ebony fingerboard, block markers; 21 frets plus zero fret; truss-rod adjuster at neck heel.
▌ Hollow archtop bound body with two f-holes; white (7593).
▌ Two humbucker pickups.
▌ Three controls (all volume) and two selectors.
▌ Colored plastic pickguard with falcon logo.
▌ Six-saddle bridge, separate vibrato tailpiece.
▌ Gold-plated hardware.
Some examples with separate frame-type tailpiece.

WHITE FALCON STEREO first version 1958-59 *Falcon logo on pickguard, two close-spaced humbucker pickups.*
▌ Bound ebony fingerboard, engraved hump-top block markers (half-moon from c1958); 21 frets (plus zero fret from c1959); truss-rod adjuster at headstock; vertical Gretsch logo on headstock (horizontal type plus model nameplate from c1958).
▌ Hollow archtop bound body with two large f-holes; white (6137).
▌ Two split-polepiece humbucker pickups (close-spaced – one at neck, one in central position).
▌ Two controls and three selectors.
▌ Colored plastic pickguard with falcon logo.

▌ Six-saddle bridge, separate G-logo tubular frame-type tailpiece.
▌ Gold-plated hardware.
Some examples with 22 frets.
Some examples with non-split-polepiece humbucker pickups.
Some examples with optional separate vibrato tailpiece.

WHITE FALCON STEREO second version 1959-62 *Falcon logo on pickguard, two controls and five selectors.*
Similar to first version, except:
▌ Two humbucker pickups.
▌ Two controls (both volume) and five selectors (plus two string damper controls from c1961).
▌ Pad on body back from c1961.
▌ Double string damper and two controls from c1961.
Succeeded by twin-cutaway third version, see listing under STYLE SIX.

WHITE FALCON STEREO fifth version 1974-78. *Falcon logo on pickguard, two controls, five selectors, block markers.*
▌ Bound ebony fingerboard, block markers; 21 frets plus zero fret; truss-rod adjuster at neck heel.
▌ Hollow archtop bound body with two f-holes; white (7593).
▌ Two humbucker pickups.
▌ Two controls and five selectors.
▌ Colored plastic pickguard with falcon logo.
▌ Six-saddle bridge, separate vibrato tailpiece.
▌ Gold-plated hardware.

WHITE FALCON I – 1955 CUSTOM 1995-current *Re-issue based on 1955-period original, but with 22 frets as standard.*

STYLE TWO (1989-current) JAPAN
One rounded cutaway on large body

ANNIVERSARY one-pickup 1993-current *Anniversary on headstock, one pickup.*

90

BODY STYLES
Each main model entry above includes a 'Style bar' to identify which of Gretsch's 20 distinctive body Styles is used. The styles are shown in silhouette, on the right, numbered 1 to 20.

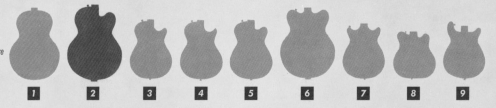

1   2   3   4   5   6   7   8   9

■ Bound ebony fingerboard, half-moon markers; 22 frets; truss-rod adjuster at headstock; model nameplate on headstock.
■ Hollow archtop bound body with two large f-holes; sunburst (6124) or light/dark green (6125).
■ One humbucker pickup.
■ One control (volume) and one selector.
■ Colored plastic pickguard.
■ Six-saddle bridge, separate G-hole flat tailpiece.

ANNIVERSARY two-pickup 1993-current *Anniversary on headstock, two pickups.*
■ Sunburst (6117) or light/dark green (6118).
■ Two humbucker pickups.
■ Three controls (all volume) and two selectors.

BLACK FALCON 6136BK 1992-current *Falcon logo on pickguard, 22 frets, G-logo tubular frame-type tailpiece, black.*
Similar to WHITE FALCON 6136, except:
■ Black (6136BK).

BLACK FALCON 7593BK 1992-current *Falcon logo on pickguard, 22 frets, vibrato tailpiece, black.*
Similar to WHITE FALCON 7593, except:
■ Black (7593BK)

BRIAN SETZER See NASHVILLE BRIAN SETZER 6120SSU listing.

COUNTRY CLASSIC I 1989-current *Country Classic I on headstock and pickguard.*
■ Bound ebony fingerboard, half-moon markers; 22 frets; truss-rod adjuster at headstock; model nameplate on headstock.
■ Hollow archtop bound body with two f-holes; dark brown (6122-S).
■ Two humbucker pickups.

■ Four controls (three volume, one tone) and one selector.
■ Colored plastic pickguard with model name.
■ Six-saddle bridge, separate vibrato tailpiece.
■ Gold-plated hardware.

NASHVILLE 6120 1989-current *Horseshoe on headstock, block markers.*
■ Bound rosewood fingerboard, block markers; 22 frets; truss-rod adjuster at headstock; horseshoe on headstock.
■ Hollow archtop bound body with two large f-holes; orange (6120).
■ Two humbucker pickups.
■ Four controls (three volume, one tone) and one selector.
■ Colored plastic pickguard.
■ Six-saddle bridge, separate vibrato tailpiece.
■ Gold-plated hardware.
Also blue sunburst (6120BS) from c1992.
Also green (6120GR) from c1993.
Also tiger maple (6120TM) from c1993.

NASHVILLE 6120-1960 1992-current *Horseshoe on headstock, half-moon markers, zero fret.*
Similar to NASHVILLE 6120, except:
■ Bound ebony fingerboard, half-moon markers; 22 frets plus zero fret.
■ Three controls (all volume) and two selectors.

NASHVILLE BRIAN SETZER 6120SSU 1993-current *Brian Setzer signature on pickguard.*
Similar to NASHVILLE 6120-1960, except:
■ 22 frets with NO zero fret; Brian Setzer on truss-rod cover.
■ Two optional dice-style control knobs.
■ Colored plastic pickguard with Brian Setzer signature and model name.
Also vintage-style cellulose lacquer (6120SSL).
Also green (6120SSUGR).

NASHVILLE WESTERN 6120W 1989-current *Horseshoe on headstock, block markers, G-logo on body front.*
Similar to NASHVILLE, except:
■ Western motif block markers.
■ Body with G-logo on front; orange (6120W).
■ Colored plastic pickguard with Nashville logo.

RANCHER 6022CV 1992-current *Steer head on headstock, triangular soundhole, one pickup.*
■ Bound ebony fingerboard, block markers; 20 frets; truss-rod adjuster at headstock; steer head on headstock.
■ Hollow flat-top bound body with triangular soundhole; orange (6022CV).
■ One single-coil pickup at neck.
■ Two controls (volume, tone) mounted on body side.
■ Six-saddle bridge, separate vibrato tailpiece.

SILVER FALCON 6136SL 1995-current *Falcon logo on pickguard, 22 frets, G-logo tubular frame-type tailpiece, black, chrome-plated hardware.*
Similar to WHITE FALCON 6136, except:
■ Black (6136SL).
■ Chrome-plated hardware.

SYNCHROMATIC 400MCV 1992-current *Synchromatic on headstock, vibrato tailpiece.*
■ Bound ebony fingerboard, split hump-top block markers; 20 frets; truss-rod adjuster at headstock; Synchromatic on headstock.
■ Hollow archtop bound body with two 'cat's-eye' soundholes; natural.
■ One humbucker pickup at neck.
■ Two controls (volume, tone) mounted on pickguard.
■ Colored elongated plastic pickguard.
■ Six-saddle bridge, separate vibrato tailpiece.

91

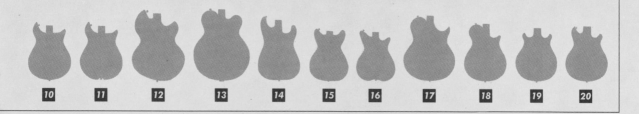

10   11   12   13   14   15   16   17   18   19   20

■ Gold-plated hardware.
Also sunburst (400CV) from c1994.

SYNCHROMATIC 6040MC-SS 1994-current
*Synchromatic on headstock, harp-frame
tailpiece.*
Similar to SYNCHROMATIC 400MCV,
except:
■ Single-saddle wooden bridge,
separate harp-frame tailpiece.

TENNESSEE ROSE 6119 1989-current
Tennessee Rose on pickguard, f-holes.
■ Bound rosewood fingerboard, half-
moon markers; 22 frets; truss-rod
adjuster at headstock.
■ Hollow archtop bound body with two
f-holes; dark red (6119).
■ Two humbucker pickups.
■ Four controls (three volume, one tone)
and one selector.
■ Colored plastic pickguard with model
name.
■ Six-saddle bridge, separate vibrato
tailpiece.

TENNESSEE ROSE 6119-1962 1993-current
*Tennessee Rose on pickguard, fake f-
holes, zero fret.*
Similar to TENNESSEE ROSE 6119,
except:
■ 22 frets plus zero fret.
■ Hollow archtop bound body with two
fake f-holes; brown (6119-1962).
■ Three controls (all volume) and three
selectors.
■ Single-saddle bridge.

WHITE FALCON 6136 1990-current *Falcon
logo on pickguard, 22 frets, G-logo
tubular frame-type tailpiece, white.*
■ Bound ebony fingerboard, hump-top
block markers; 22 frets; truss-rod
adjuster at headstock; vertical Gretsch
logo on headstock.
■ Hollow archtop bound body with two
large f-holes; white (6136).
■ Two humbucker pickups.
■ Four controls (three volume, one tone)

and one selector.
■ Colored plastic pickguard with falcon
logo.
■ Six-saddle bridge, separate G-logo
tubular frame-type tailpiece.
■ Gold-plated hardware.
*Some early examples with block
markers, horizontal Gretsch logo on
headstock, two f-holes.*

WHITE FALCON 7593 1990-current *Falcon
logo on pickguard, 22 frets, vibrato
tailpiece, white.*
Similar to WHITE FALCON 6136,
except:
■ Block markers; horizontal Gretsch
logo on headstock.
■ Two f-holes; white (7593).
■ Separate vibrato tailpiece.

<hr>

STYLE THREE (1953-79) USA

One semi-pointed cutaway on small body

CHET ATKINS SOLID BODY first version 1955-
61 *Chet Atkins logo on pickguard,
single-saddle bridge.*
■ Bound rosewood fingerboard (ebony
from c1958), engraved block markers
(plain block from c1956; hump-top
block from c1957; half-moon from
c1958); 22 frets (plus zero fret from
c1959); truss-rod adjuster at headstock;
steer head on headstock (horseshoe
from c1956).
■ Semi-solid bound body with G-brand
on front (no G-brand from c1957);
studded leather around sides (c1954-
56); orange front (6121).
■ Two single-coil pickups (two
humbucker pickups from c1958).
■ Four controls (three volume, one tone)
and one selector (three controls – all
volume – and two selectors from
c1958).
■ Colored plastic pickguard with Chet
Atkins logo.
■ Single-saddle bridge, separate vibrato
tailpiece.

■ Gold-plated hardware.
*Succeeded by twin-cutaway second
version, see listing under STYLE SEVEN.*

COUNTRY ROC 1974-79 *Orange body
front, five controls and one selector, G-
brand on body front.*
■ Bound ebony fingerboard, western
motif block markers; 22 frets plus zero
fret; truss-rod adjuster at neck heel;
horseshoe on headstock.
■ Semi-solid bound body with G-brand
on front; studded leather around sides;
orange front (7620).
■ Two humbucker pickups.
■ Five controls (three volume, two tone)
and one selector.
■ Colored plastic pickguard.
■ Six-saddle bridge, separate G-hole
tailpiece with western-style belt buckle.
■ Gold-plated hardware.

DUO JET first version 1953-61 *Black body
front.*
■ Bound rosewood fingerboard, block
markers (hump-top block from c1957;
half-moon from c1958); 22 frets (plus
zero fret from c1959); truss-rod adjuster
at headstock.
■ Semi-solid bound body; black front
(6128).
■ Two single-coil pickups (two
humbucker pickups from c1958).
■ Four controls (three volume, one tone)
and one selector (three controls – all
volume – and two selectors from
c1958).
■ Colored plastic pickguard.
■ Six-saddle bridge, separate G-hole
flat tailpiece or vibrato tailpiece.
*Some examples with green body-front
and gold-plated hardware (6128).
Succeeded by twin-cutaway second
version, see listing under STYLE SEVEN.*

JET FIRE BIRD first version 1955-61 *Red
body front.*
Similar to DUO JET first version, except:
■ Black with red body front (6131).

92

BODY STYLES
*Each main model entry above
includes a 'Style bar' to identify
which of Gretsch's 20 distinctive
body Styles is used. The styles are
shown in silhouette, on the right,
numbered 1 to 20.*

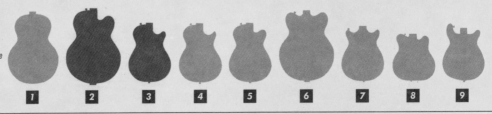

Some examples with 21 frets. *Succeeded by twin-cutaway second version, see listing under STYLE SEVEN.*

ROC II 1973-75 *Dark red, all controls on elliptical plate.*
▌ Bound ebony fingerboard, half-moon markers; 22 frets plus zero fret; truss-rod adjuster at neck heel.
▌ Solid bound body; dark red (7621).
▌ Two humbucker pickups.
▌ Four controls (two volume, treble boost, distortion) and two selectors, all on elliptical plate; active circuit.
▌ Six-saddle bridge/tailpiece.

ROC JET first version 1969-72 *Roc Jet on headstock.*
▌ Bound ebony fingerboard, half-moon markers; 22 frets plus zero fret; truss-rod adjuster at headstock; model nameplate on headstock.
▌ Semi-solid bound body; orange front (6127) or black front (6130).
▌ Two humbucker pickups.
▌ Colored plastic pickguard.
▌ Five controls (three volume, two tone) and one selector.
▌ Six-saddle bridge, separate G-hole flat tailpiece.

ROC JET second version 1972-79 *Various color body fronts, truss-rod adjuster at neck heel, chrome-plated hardware.*
Similar to first version, except:
▌ Bound rosewood fingerboard from c1977; truss-rod adjuster at neck heel; no model nameplate on headstock.
▌ Black front (7610) (7611 from c1977), orange front (7611) c1971-74, red front (7612) c1972-77, or brown front (7613) c1972-77.
▌ Six-saddle wrapover bridge/tailpiece from c1977.

ROUND UP 1954-59 *Orange body front, four controls and one selector, steer head logo on pickguard.*
▌ Bound rosewood fingerboard,

engraved block markers; 22 frets; truss-rod adjuster at headstock; steer head on headstock.
▌ Semi-solid bound body with G-brand on front; studded leather around sides; orange front (6130).
▌ Two single-coil pickups.
▌ Four controls (three volume, one tone) and one selector.
▌ Tortoiseshell or colored plastic pickguard with steer head logo.
▌ Six-saddle bridge, separate G-hole flat tailpiece with western-style belt buckle.
▌ Gold-plated hardware.

SILVER JET first version 1954-61 *Silver sparkle body front.*
Similar to DUO JET first version, except:
▌ Silver sparkle body-front (6129).
Succeeded by twin-cutaway second version, see listing under STYLE SEVEN.

WHITE PENGUIN first version 1955-61 *Penguin logo on pickguard.*
▌ Bound ebony fingerboard, engraved hump-top block markers (half-moon from c1958); 22 frets; truss-rod adjuster at headstock; vertical Gretsch logo on headstock (horizontal type from c1958).
▌ Semi-solid bound body; white (6134).
▌ Two single-coil pickups (two humbucker pickups from c1958).
▌ Four controls (three volume, one tone) and one selector (three controls – all volume – and two selectors from c1958).
▌ Colored plastic pickguard with penguin logo.
▌ Six-saddle bridge, separate G-logo tubular frame tailpiece.
▌ Gold-plated hardware.
▌ Metal arm-rest.
Some examples in black and white, or with gold sparkle body front. Some examples without metal arm-rest. Succeeded by twin-cutaway second version, see listing under STYLE SEVEN.

One semi-pointed cutaway on small body

DUO JET 6128 1989-current *Black body front, two humbucker pickups.*
▌ Bound rosewood fingerboard, hump-top block markers; 22 frets; truss-rod adjuster at headstock; horseshoe on headstock.
▌ Semi-solid bound body; black front (6128).
▌ Two humbucker pickups.
▌ Four controls (three volume, one tone) and one selector.
▌ Colored plastic pickguard
▌ Six-saddle bridge, separate G-hole flat tailpiece.
Also DUO JET 6128T with separate vibrato tailpiece from c1994.

DUO JET 6128-1957 1994-current *Black body front, two single-coil pickups.*
Similar to DUO JET 6128, except:
▌ No horseshoe on headstock.
▌ Two single-coil pickups.
Also DUO JET 6128T-1957 with separate vibrato tailpiece.

JET FIREBIRD 1989-current *Red body front, two humbucker pickups.*
Similar to DUO JET 6128, except:
▌ Red body front (6131).
▌ Gold-plated hardware.

ROUND UP 1989-current *G-logo on orange body front, two humbucker pickups.*
Similar to DUO JET 6128, except:
▌ Western motif block markers.
▌ G-logo on orange body front (6121).
▌ Separate vibrato tailpiece,
▌ Gold-plated hardware.

SILVER JET 6129 1989-current *Silver sparkle body front, two humbucker pickups.*
Similar to DUO JET 6128, except:
▌ Silver sparkle body front (6129).

93

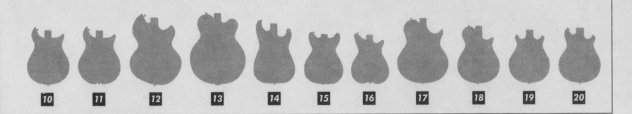

10   11   12   13   14   15   16   17   18   19   20

Also *SILVER JET 6129T with separate vibrato tailpiece from c1994.*

SILVER JET 6129-1957 1994-current *Silver sparkle body front, two single-coil pickups.*
Similar to DUO JET 6128, except:
■ No horseshoe on headstock.
■ Silver sparkle body front.
■ Two single-coil pickups.
Also SILVER JET 6129T-1957 with separate vibrato tailpiece.

SPARKLE JET 6129 1995-current *Blue pearl or various color sparkle body fronts (NOT silver), two humbucker pickups.*
Similar to DUO JET 6128, except:
■ Blue pearl or various color sparkle body fronts (NOT silver).
Also SPARKLE JET 6129T with separate vibrato tailpiece.

SPARKLE JET 6129-1957 1995-current *Blue pearl or various color sparkle body fronts (NOT silver), two single-coil pickups.*
Similar to DUO JET 6128, except:
■ No horseshoe on headstock.
■ Blue pearl or various color sparkle body fronts (NOT silver).
■ Two single-coil pickups.
Also SPARKLE JET 6129T-1957 with separate vibrato tailpiece.

94

WHITE PENGUIN 1993-94 *White, penguin logo on pickguard.*
■ Bound ebony fingerboard, feather motif hump-top block markers; 22 frets; truss-rod adjuster at headstock; vertical Gretsch logo on headstock.
■ Semi-solid bound body; white (6134).
■ Two single-coil pickups.
■ Four controls (three volume, one tone) and one selector.
■ Colored plastic pickguard with penguin logo.
■ Six-saddle bridge, separate G-logo tubular frame tailpiece.
■ Gold-plated hardware.

STYLE FOUR (1957-60) USA
One sharp-pointed cutaway on small body

RAMBLER first version 1957-60 *One sharp-pointed cutaway and two large f-holes on small body.*
■ Unbound rosewood fingerboard, dot markers; 20 frets; truss-rod adjuster at headstock.
■ Hollow archtop bound body with two large f-holes; cream/black (6115).
■ One single-coil pickup at neck.
■ Two controls (volume, tone).
■ Colored plastic pickguard.
■ Single-saddle wooden bridge, separate G-hole flat tailpiece.
Some examples in cream/green (6115). Succeeded by rounded-cutaway second version, see listing under STYLE FIVE.

STYLE FIVE (1960-62) USA
One rounded cutaway on small body

RAMBLER second version 1960-62 *One rounded cutaway and two large f-holes on small body.*
■ Unbound rosewood fingerboard, dot markers; 20 frets; truss-rod adjuster at headstock.
■ Hollow archtop bound body with two large f-holes; cream/black (6115).
■ One single-coil pickup at neck.
■ Two controls (volume, tone).
■ Colored plastic pickguard.
■ Single-saddle wooden bridge, separate G-hole flat tailpiece.
Some examples in cream/green (6115). Succeeded sharp-pointed cutaway first version, see listing under STYLE FOUR.

STYLE SIX (1961-81) USA
Twin shallow cutaways on large body

BLACK HAWK 1967-70 *Black Hawk on headstock.*

■ Bound rosewood fingerboard, half-moon markers with dot markers from 15th fret; 22 frets plus zero fret; truss-rod adjuster at headstock; model nameplate on headstock.
■ Hollow archtop bound body with two f-holes; sunburst (6100) c1967-70, or black (6101).
■ Two humbucker pickups.
■ Three controls (all volume) and three selectors.
■ Colored plastic pickguard.
■ Bar-frame 'Floating Sound' unit plus six-saddle bridge, separate G-hole flat tailpiece.

BROADKASTER semi-hollow body first version 1975-77 *Dot markers, three controls and two selectors.*
■ Unbound rosewood fingerboard, dot markers; 22 frets plus zero fret; truss-rod adjuster at headstock.
■ Semi-hollow bound body with two f-holes; natural (7607) or sunburst (7608).
■ Two humbucker pickups.
■ Three controls (all volume) and two selectors.
■ Colored plastic pickguard.
■ Six-saddle bridge/tailpiece.
Also in natural (7603) or sunburst (7604) with six-saddle bridge, separate vibrato tailpiece.

BROADKASTER semi-hollow body second version 1977-79 *Dot markers, five controls and one selector.*
Similar to first version, except:
■ Red only (7609).
■ Five controls (three volume, two tone) and one selector.
■ Six-saddle wrapover bridge/tailpiece.

CHET ATKINS COUNTRY GENTLEMAN second version 1961-72 *Chet Atkins Country Gentleman on headstock, fake f-holes.*
■ Bound ebony fingerboard, half-moon markers; 22 frets plus zero fret; truss-rod adjuster at headstock; model

BODY STYLES
Each main model entry above includes a 'Style bar' to identify which of Gretsch's 20 distinctive body Styles is used. The styles are shown in silhouette, on the right, numbered 1 to 20.

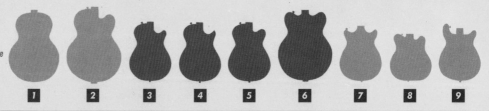

nameplate on headstock.
∎ Hollow archtop bound body with two fake f-holes; dark brown (6122).
∎ Two humbucker pickups.
∎ Three controls (all volume) and three selectors, plus one or two string damper controls.
∎ Colored plastic pickguard (with model name from c1967).
∎ Single-saddle bridge, separate vibrato tailpiece.
∎ Gold-plated hardware.
∎ Pad on body back.
∎ Double string damper and two controls (single string damper and one control from c1966).
Some examples with f-holes.
Some examples in black from c1967.
Succeeded single-cutaway first version, see listing under STYLE TWO.

CHET ATKINS COUNTRY GENTLEMAN third version 1972-81 *Chet Atkins Country Gentleman on pickguard, f-holes.*
Similar to second version, except:
∎ Truss-rod adjuster at neck heel; no model nameplate on headstock.
∎ Hollow archtop body with two f-holes; brown (7670).
∎ Three controls (all volume) and two selectors from c1978.
∎ Six-saddle bridge.
∎ No pad on body back.
∎ No string damper and control.
Known as COUNTRY SQUIRE (7676) from c1981.

CHET ATKINS HOLLOW BODY second version
1961-67 *Chet Atkins logo on pickguard, fake f-holes, orange.*
∎ Bound ebony fingerboard, half-moon markers; 22 frets plus zero fret; truss-rod adjuster at headstock; horseshoe on headstock.
∎ Hollow archtop bound body with two fake f-holes; orange (6120).
∎ Two humbucker pickups.
∎ Three controls (all volume) and three selectors, plus string damper control.

∎ Colored plastic pickguard with Chet Atkins name.
∎ Single-saddle bridge, separate vibrato tailpiece.
∎ Gold-plated hardware.
∎ Pad on body back.
∎ String damper and control.
Succeeded single-cutaway first version, see listing under STYLE TWO.
Known as CHET ATKINS NASHVILLE from c1967, see separate listing.

CHET ATKINS NASHVILLE first version 1967-72 *Chet Atkins Nashville on headstock and pickguard, fake f-holes.*
Similar to CHET ATKINS HOLLOW BODY second version, except:
∎ Model nameplate on headstock.
∎ Model name on pickguard.
Some examples with bound rosewood fingerboard.
Previously known as CHET ATKINS HOLLOW BODY second version, see separate listing.

CHET ATKINS NASHVILLE second version
1972-79 *Chet Atkins Nashville on pickguard only, f-holes.*
Similar to CHET ATKINS HOLLOW BODY second version, except:
∎ Truss-rod adjuster at neck heel; no horseshoe or model nameplate on headstock.
∎ Hollow archtop bound body with two f-holes; red (7660).
∎ Three controls (all volume) and two selectors from c1978.
∎ Colored plastic pickguard with model name.
∎ Six-saddle bridge.
∎ No pad on body back.
∎ No string damper and control.

COUNTRY GENTLEMAN See CHET ATKINS COUNTRY GENTLEMAN listings.

COUNTRY SQUIRE See CHET ATKINS COUNTRY GENTLEMAN third version listing.

HOLLOW BODY See CHET ATKINS HOLLOW BODY second version listing.

MONKEES 1966-1967 *Monkees on truss-rod cover and pickguard.*
∎ Bound rosewood fingerboard, left and right half-moon markers; 22 frets plus zero fret; truss-rod adjuster at headstock; model nameplate on headstock; Monkees logo on truss-rod cover.
∎ Hollow archtop bound body with two f-holes; red (6123).
∎ Two humbucker pickups.
∎ Three controls (all volume) and three selectors.
∎ Colored plastic pickguard with Monkees logo.
∎ Single-saddle bridge, separate vibrato tailpiece.

NASHVILLE See CHET ATKINS NASHVILLE listings.

RALLY 1967-68 *Half-moon/dot markers, diagonal stripes on truss-rod cover and pickguard.*
∎ Bound rosewood fingerboard, half-moon markers with dot markers from 15th fret; 22 frets plus zero fret; truss-rod adjuster at headstock; diagonal stripes on truss-rod cover.
∎ Hollow archtop bound body with two f-holes; green (6104) or yellow/brown (6105).
∎ Two single-coil pickups.
∎ Four controls (three volume, treble boost) and three selectors; active circuit.
∎ Colored plastic pickguard with diagonal stripes.
∎ Single-saddle bridge, separate vibrato tailpiece.
Some examples with six-saddle bridge.

RONNY LEE 1962-63 *Ronny Lee on headstock, large fake f-holes.*
∎ Bound rosewood fingerboard, left and right half-moon markers; 22 frets plus zero fret; truss-rod adjuster at

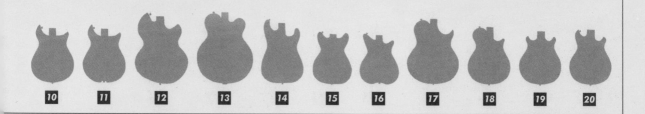

10 11 12 13 14 15 16 17 18 19 20

headstock; model nameplate on headstock.
■ Hollow archtop bound body with two large fake f-holes; sunburst or brown.
■ Two single-coil pickups.
■ Three controls (all volume) and three selectors.
■ Colored plastic pickguard.
■ Six-saddle bridge, separate vibrato tailpiece.
Some examples with single-saddle bridge.

SAM GOODY 1967 *Sam Goody on headstock, G-shape soundholes.*
■ Bound rosewood fingerboard, half-moon markers with dot markers from 15th fret; 22 frets plus zero fret; truss-rod adjuster at headstock; model nameplate on headstock.
■ Hollow archtop bound body with two G-shape soundholes; sunburst.
■ Two single-coil pickups.
■ Three controls (all volume) and three selectors.
■ Colored plastic pickguard.
■ Single-saddle bridge, separate vibrato tailpiece.

STREAMLINER second version 1968-72 *Streamliner on headstock.*
■ Bound rosewood fingerboard, half-moon markers with dot markers from 15th fret; 22 frets plus zero fret; truss-rod adjuster at headstock; model nameplate on headstock.
■ Hollow archtop bound body with two f-holes; sunburst (6102) or red (6103).
■ Two humbucker pickups.
■ Three controls (all volume) and three selectors.
■ Colored plastic pickguard.
■ Six-saddle bridge, separate G-hole flat tailpiece.

STREAMLINER third version 1972-75 *Half-moon markers, truss-rod adjuster at neck heel, G-hole flat tailpiece.*
Similar to first version, except:

■ Half-moon markers (all); truss-rod adjuster at neck heel; no model nameplate on headstock.
■ Sunburst (7565) c1972-73, or red (7566).

VIKING first version 1964-72 *Viking on headstock and pickguard.*
■ Bound ebony fingerboard, half-moon markers with offset dot markers from 15th fret; 21 frets plus zero fret; truss-rod adjuster at headstock; model nameplate on headstock.
■ Hollow archtop bound body with two large f-holes; sunburst (6187), natural (6188) or green (6189).
■ Two humbucker pickups.
■ Three controls (all volume) and three selectors, plus one string damper control.
■ Colored plastic pickguard with model name.
■ Six-saddle bridge (bar-frame 'Floating Sound' unit plus six-saddle bridge from c1966), separate vibrato tailpiece.
■ Gold-plated hardware.
■ Pad on body back.
■ String damper and control.
Some early examples with Viking ship logo and model name on pickguard.

VIKING second version 1972-74 *Viking on pickguard only, truss-rod adjuster at neck heel.*
Similar to first version, except:
■ Truss-rod adjuster at neck heel; no model nameplate on headstock.
■ Hollow archtop body with two f-holes; sunburst (7585) or natural (7586).
■ No pad on body back.
■ No string damper and control.

WHITE FALCON second version 1962-72
White Falcon on headstock, falcon logo on pickguard.
■ Bound ebony fingerboard, half-moon markers (with offset dot markers from 15th fret from c1964); 21 frets plus

zero fret; truss-rod adjuster at headstock; model nameplate on headstock.
■ Hollow archtop bound body with two large f-holes; white (6136).
■ Two humbucker pickups.
■ Three controls (all volume) and three selectors, plus two string damper controls.
■ Colored plastic pickguard with falcon logo.
■ Six-saddle bridge (bar-frame 'Floating Sound' unit plus six-saddle bridge from c1966), separate G-logo tubular frame tailpiece (separate vibrato tailpiece from c1964).
■ Gold-plated hardware.
■ Pad on body back.
■ Double string damper and two controls.
Some examples with three controls (all volume) and two selectors.
Vibrato tailpiece option c1962-64.
Succeeded single-cutaway first version, see listing under STYLE TWO.

WHITE FALCON third version 1972-80
Falcon logo on pickguard, truss-rod adjuster at neck heel.
Similar to second version, except:
■ Block position markers from c1974; truss-rod adjuster at neck heel; no model nameplate on headstock.
■ Hollow archtop bound body with two f-holes; white (7594).
■ Three controls (all volume) and two selectors from c1978.
■ Six-saddle bridge from c1974.
■ No double string damper and two controls from c1974.
Some examples with two large f-holes.

WHITE FALCON STEREO third version 1962-72
White Falcon on headstock, falcon logo on pickguard, two controls and five or six selectors.
■ Bound ebony fingerboard, half-moon markers (with offset dot markers from 15th fret from c1964); 21 frets plus

96

BODY STYLES
Each main model entry above includes a 'Style bar' to identify which of Gretsch's 20 distinctive body Styles is used. The styles are shown in silhouette, on the right, numbered 1 to 20.

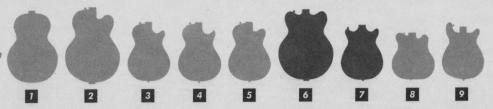

1 2 3 4 5 6 7 8 9

zero fret; truss-rod adjuster at headstock; model nameplate on headstock.
- Hollow archtop bound body with two large f-holes; white (6137).
- Two humbucker pickups.
- Two controls (both volume) and six selectors (two controls – both volume – and five selectors, all on right body front, from c1965; two controls – both volume – and six selectors, including one on lower left body front, from c1966), plus two string damper controls.
- Colored plastic pickguard with falcon logo.
- Six-saddle bridge (bar-frame 'Floating Sound' unit plus six-saddle bridge from c1966), separate G-logo tubular frame tailpiece (separate vibrato tailpiece from c1964).
- Gold-plated hardware.
- Pad on body back.
- Double string damper and two controls.
Vibrato tailpiece option c1962-64. Some examples with two controls (both volume) and five selectors, plus two string damper controls c1962-65. Succeeded single-cutaway second version, see listing under STYLE TWO.

WHITE FALCON STEREO fourth version 1972-81 *Falcon logo on pickguard, truss-rod adjuster at neck heel, two controls and five or six selectors.*
Similar to WHITE FALCON STEREO third version, except:
- Block position markers from c1974; truss-rod adjuster at neck heel; no model nameplate on headstock.
- Hollow archtop bound body with two f-holes; white (7595).
- Two controls (both volume) and six selectors (two controls – both volume – and five selectors from c1978), plus two string damper controls c1972-74.
- Six-saddle bridge from c1974.
- No double string damper and two controls from c1974.

Some examples with two large f-holes.

12-STRING 1966-70 *Triangular markers, 12-string headstock.*
- Bound rosewood or ebony fingerboard, triangle markers; 22 frets plus zero fret; truss-rod adjuster at headstock; 12-string headstock.
- Hollow archtop bound body with two large f-holes; sunburst (6075) or natural (6076).
- Two humbucker pickups.
- Three controls (all volume) and three selectors.
- Colored plastic pickguard.
- Single-saddle wooden bridge, separate G-hole flat tailpiece.
Some examples with pad on body back. Some examples with string damper and control.

STYLE SIX (1989-current) JAPAN
Twin shallow cutaways on large body

BLACK FALCON 7594BK 1992-current *Falcon logo on pickguard, 22 frets, black.*
Similar to WHITE FALCON 7594, except:
- Black (7594BK).

COUNTRY CLASSIC II 6122 1989-current *Country Classic II on headstock and pickguard, f-holes.*
- Bound ebony fingerboard, half-moon markers; 22 frets; truss-rod adjuster at headstock; model nameplate on headstock.
- Hollow archtop bound body with two f-holes; dark brown (6122).
- Two humbucker pickups.
- Four controls (three volume, one tone) and one selector.
- Colored plastic pickguard with model name.
- Six-saddle bridge, separate vibrato tailpiece.
- Gold-plated hardware.

COUNTRY CLASSIC II 6122-1962 1993-current *Country Classic II on headstock and pickguard, fake f-holes, zero fret.*
Similar to COUNTRY CLASSIC 6122, except:
- 22 frets plus zero fret.
- Hollow archtop bound body with two fake f-holes.
- Three controls (all volume) and three selectors.
- Single-saddle bridge.

SILVER FALCON 7594SL 1995-current *Falcon logo on pickguard, 22 frets, black, chrome-plated hardware.*
Similar to WHITE FALCON 7594, except:
- Black (7594SL).
- Chrome-plated hardware.

WHITE FALCON 7594 1990-current *Falcon logo on pickguard, 22 frets, white.*
- Bound ebony fingerboard, block markers; 22 frets; truss-rod adjuster at headstock.
- Hollow archtop bound body with two f-holes; white (7594).
- Two humbucker pickups.
- Four controls (three volume, one tone) and one selector.
- Colored plastic pickguard with falcon logo.
- Six-saddle bridge, separate vibrato tailpiece.
- Gold-plated hardware.

STYLE SEVEN (1961-69) USA
Twin semi-pointed cutaways on small body

CHET ATKINS SOLID BODY second version 1961-62 *Orange body front, Chet Atkins logo on pickguard.*
- Bound ebony fingerboard, half-moon markers; 22 frets plus zero fret; truss-rod adjuster at headstock; horseshoe on headstock.
- Semi-solid bound body; orange front (6121).

97

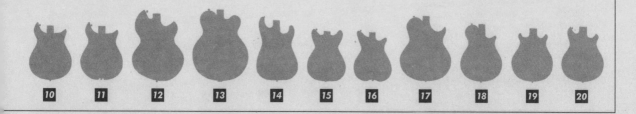

10   11   12   13   14   15   16   17   18   19   20

- Two humbucker pickups.
- Three controls (all volume) and two selectors (three controls – all volume – and three selectors from c1962).
- Colored plastic pickguard with Chet Atkins logo.
- Single-saddle bridge, separate vibrato tailpiece.
- Gold-plated hardware.
Succeeded single-cutaway first version, see listing under STYLE THREE.

DUO JET second version 1961-69 *Black body front.*
- Bound rosewood fingerboard, half-moon markers; 22 frets plus zero fret; truss-rod adjuster at headstock.
- Semi-solid bound body; black front (6128).
- Two humbucker pickups.
- Three controls (all volume) and two selectors (three controls – all volume – and three selectors from c1962; four controls – three volume, treble boost – and three selectors from c1968).
- Colored plastic pickguard.
- Six-saddle bridge, separate vibrato tailpiece.
- Gold-plated hardware from c1962.
Some examples with G-hole flat tailpiece.
Also with various color sparkle body fronts from c1963, previously known as SILVER JET second version, see separate listing.
Succeeded single-cutaway first version, see listing under STYLE THREE.

JET FIRE BIRD second version 1961-69 *Red body front.*
Similar to DUO JET second version, except:
- Black with red body front (6131).
Some examples with 21 frets.
Succeeded single-cutaway first version, see listing under STYLE THREE.

SILVER JET second version 1961-63 *Silver sparkle body front.*

Similar to DUO JET second version, except:
- Silver sparkle body front (6129).
Also other color sparkle body front options from c1962.
Known as DUO JET second version with various color sparkle body fronts from c1963, see separate listing.
Succeeded single-cutaway first version, see listing under STYLE THREE.

WHITE PENGUIN second version 1961-62 *White.*
- Bound ebony fingerboard, half-moon markers; 22 frets plus zero fret; truss-rod adjuster at headstock.
- Semi-solid bound body; white (6134).
- Two humbucker pickups.
- Three controls (all volume) and two selectors (three controls – all volume – and three selectors from c1962).
- Colored plastic pickguard with penguin logo.
- Six-saddle bridge, separate vibrato tailpiece.
- Gold-plated hardware.
Some examples without penguin logo on pickguard.
Succeeded single-cutaway first version, see listing under STYLE THREE.

STYLE EIGHT (1961) USA
Slightly-offset rounded cutaways on small body

BIKINI 1961 *Solid body with detachable slide-on hinged back section.*
- Unbound maple fingerboard, dot markers; 22 frets; truss-rod adjuster at body.
- Solid rectangular body center section with detachable slide-on hinged back; black (6023).
- One single-coil pickup.
- Two controls (volume, tone), mounted on edge of body center section.
- Wooden single-saddle bridge, separate trapeze tailpiece.

Some examples with zero fret.
Some examples with model name on headstock.
Some examples with colored plastic pickguard.
Also guitar/bass double-neck (6025).

STYLE NINE (1961-62) USA
Two rounded cutaways (with longer left horn) on small body

CORVETTE solidbody first version 1961-62
Slab body, one pickup.
- Unbound rosewood fingerboard, dot markers; 21 frets; truss-rod adjuster at body.
- Solid slab unbound body; dark brown (6132) or gray (6133).
- One single-coil pickup at bridge.
- Two controls (volume, tone) on pickguard.
- Colored plastic pickguard.
- Wooden single-saddle bridge, separate trapeze tailpiece.
Succeeded by solidbody second version, see listing under STYLE TEN.

STYLE TEN (1962-65) USA
Two pointed cutaways (with long left horn) on small body

CORVETTE solidbody second version one-pickup
1962-65 *Beveled-edge body, one pickup.*
- Unbound rosewood fingerboard, dot markers; 21 frets; truss-rod adjuster at body (truss-rod adjuster at headstock from c1962).
- Solid beveled-edge unbound body; dark red.
- One single-coil pickup at bridge.
- Two controls (volume, tone) on pickguard.
- Colored plastic pickguard.
- Single-saddle bridge, separate trapeze tailpiece (6132) or separate vibrato tailpiece (6134).

98

BODY STYLES
Each main model entry above includes a 'Style bar' to identify which of Gretsch's 20 distinctive body Styles is used. The styles are shown in silhouette, on the right, numbered 1 to 20.

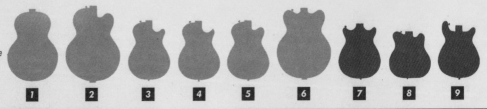

Succeeded solidbody first version, see listing under STYLE NINE.
Succeeded by solidbody third version, see listing under STYLE ELEVEN.

CORVETTE solidbody second version two-pickup
1963-65 Beveled-edge body, two pickups.
Similar to CORVETTE solidbody first version one-pickup, except:
■ Two single-coil pickups.
■ Three controls (two volume, one tone) and three-way selector, all on pickguard.
■ Single-saddle bridge, separate vibrato tailpiece (6135).
Succeeded by solidbody third version, see listing under STYLE ELEVEN.

PRINCESS *1962-63 Beveled-edge body, one pickup, pad on body back.*
Similar to CORVETTE solidbody second version one-pickup, except:
■ Blue, pink or white (all 6106).
■ Colored plastic pickguard with model name.
■ Single-saddle bridge, separate trapeze tailpiece.
■ Gold-plated hardware.
■ Pad on body back.
■ Clip-on vibrato lever.
Some examples with no model name on pickguard.

TWIST *1962-63 Beveled-edge body, one pickup, red/white striped pickguard.*
Similar to CORVETTE solidbody second version one-pickup, except:
■ Truss-rod adjuster at body.
■ Red.
■ Colored stripe plastic pickguard.
■ Separate trapeze tailpiece and clip-on vibrato lever (6109) or separate vibrato tailpiece (6110).
Some examples in yellow.

STYLE ELEVEN (1965-70) USA

Two pointed cutaways (with long left horn) on small body with cut-out in base.

CORVETTE solidbody third version one-pickup
1965-68 Two and four tuners-per-side headstock, one pickup.
■ Unbound rosewood fingerboard, dot markers; 21 frets; truss-rod adjuster at headstock; two and four tuners-per-side headstock.
■ Solid beveled-edge body; red sunburst.
■ One single-coil pickup.
■ Two controls (volume, tone) on pickguard.
■ Colored plastic pickguard.
■ Single-saddle bridge, separate trapeze tailpiece (6132) or separate vibrato tailpiece (6134).
Succeeded solidbody second version, see listing under STYLE TEN.

CORVETTE solidbody third version two-pickup
1965-70 Two and four tuners-per-side headstock, two pickups.
Similar to CORVETTE solidbody third version one-pickup, except:
■ Two single-coil pickups.
■ Three controls (two volume, one tone) and one selector (three controls – two volume, one tone – and two selectors from c1968), all on pickguard.
■ Single-saddle bridge, separate vibrato tailpiece (6135).
Some examples in gold or silver metallic finish 1966.
Succeeded solidbody second version, see listing under STYLE TEN.

'GOLD DUKE' See Corvette solidbody third version two-pickup listing.

'SILVER DUKE' See Corvette solidbody third version two-pickup listing.

STYLE TWELVE (1963-66) USA

Offset pointed cutaways on asymmetrically curved large body

ASTRO-JET *1963-66 Astro-Jet on red/black body, four and two tuners-per-side headstock.*
■ Bound ebony fingerboard, half-moon markers; 22 frets plus zero fret; truss-rod adjuster at headstock; four and two tuners-per-side headstock.
■ Solid beveled-edge unbound body with model nameplate on front; red/black (6126).
■ Two humbucker pickups.
■ Three controls (all volume) and three selectors, all on pickguard.
■ Colored plastic pickguard.
■ Six-saddle bridge, separate vibrato tailpiece.
Some examples with 21 frets. Some examples with single-saddle bridge. Some examples with string tension bar.

STYLE THIRTEEN (1972-79) USA

One rounded cutaway (and angled-in left upper bout) on large body

DELUXE CHET *1972-73 Chet Atkins on pickguard, controls on body.*
■ Bound ebony fingerboard, half-moon markers; 22 frets plus zero fret; truss-rod adjuster at neck heel.
■ Hollow archtop bound body with two f-holes; dark red (7680) or dark brown (7681).
■ Two humbucker pickups.
■ Five controls (three volume, two tone) and one selector.
■ Colored plastic pickguard with Chet Atkins name.
■ Six-saddle bridge, separate vibrato tailpiece.
■ Gold-plated hardware.

SUPER CHET *1972-79 Super Chet on pickguard with controls along edge.*

99

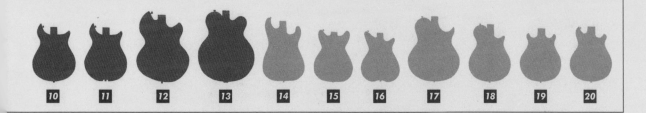

▌ Bound ebony fingerboard, floral-style markers; 22 frets plus zero fret; truss-rod adjuster at neck heel; floral-style inlay on headstock.
▌ Hollow archtop bound body with two f-holes; dark red (7690) or dark brown (7691).
▌ Two humbucker pickups.
▌ Five controls (three volume, two tone) all mounted along edge of pickguard and one selector.
▌ Colored plastic pickguard with model name.
▌ Six-saddle bridge, separate frame-type tailpiece with floral-style insert (separate vibrato tailpiece option from c1977).
▌ Gold-plated hardware.

STYLE FOURTEEN (1975-76) USA

Offset rounded cutaways on small body

BROADKASTER solidbody version 1975-76 *Two pickups, all controls and jack on pickguard.*
▌ Bolt-on neck with unbound maple fingerboard, dot markers; 22 frets; truss-rod adjuster at headstock.
▌ Solid contoured unbound body; natural (7600) or sunburst (7601).
▌ Two humbucker pickups.
▌ Two controls (both volume), two selectors and jack, all on pickguard.
▌ Colored plastic pickguard.
▌ Six-saddle bridge/tailpiece.

STYLE FIFTEEN (1977-81) USA

Twin rounded cutaways on small body

COMMITTEE 1977-81 *22-fret laminated through-neck.*
▌ Laminated through-neck with bound rosewood fingerboard, dot markers; 22 frets; truss-rod adjuster at neck heel.
▌ Solid contoured unbound body; brown (7628).

▌ Two humbucker pickups.
▌ Four controls (two volume, two tone) and one selector.
▌ Clear plastic pickguard.
▌ Six-saddle bridge/tailpiece with through-body stringing.
Some examples with colored plastic pickguard.

STYLE SIXTEEN (1977-81) USA

Offset semi-pointed cutaways on small body with curved cut-out in base

TK 300 1977-81 *Six tuners-in-line headstock.*
▌ Bolt-on neck with unbound rosewood fingerboard, dot markers; 22 frets; truss-rod adjuster at neck heel; six tuners-in-line headstock with long Gretsch logo.
▌ Solid unbound body; red (7624) or natural (7625).
▌ Two humbucker pickups.
▌ Two controls (volume, tone) and one selector, all on pickguard.
▌ Colored plastic pickguard.
▌ Six-saddle wrapover bridge/tailpiece.

STYLE SEVENTEEN (1977-80) USA

One sharp-pointed cutaway (and angled-in left upper bout) on large body

ATKINS AXE 1977-80 *Small block markers, controls on body.*
▌ Bound ebony fingerboard, small position markers; 22 frets plus zero fret; truss-rod adjuster at neck heel.
▌ Solid bound body; dark gray (7685) or red (7686).
▌ Two humbucker pickups.
▌ Four controls (two volume, two tone) and one selector.
▌ Colored plastic pickguard.
▌ Six-saddle wrapover bridge/tailpiece.

SUPER AXE 1977-80 *Small block markers, controls on elliptical plate.*

▌ Bound ebony fingerboard, small block markers; 22 frets plus zero fret; truss-rod adjuster at neck heel.
▌ Solid bound body; red (7680), dark gray (7681) or sunburst (7682).
▌ Two humbucker pickups.
▌ Five controls (volume, tone, sustain, phaser blend, phaser rate), two selectors and jack, all on elliptical plate; one selector on body; active circuit.
▌ Colored plastic pickguard.
▌ Six-saddle wrapover bridge/tailpiece.

STYLE SEVENTEEN (1995-current) JAPAN

One sharp-pointed cutaway (and angled-in left upper bout) on large body

AXE 1995-current *Small block markers, controls on body, truss-rod adjuster at headstock.*
▌ Bound rosewood fingerboard, small block markers; 22 frets; truss-rod adjuster at headstock.
▌ Solid bound body; dark red (7685).
▌ Two humbucker pickups.
▌ Four controls (two volume, two tone) and one selector.
▌ Colored plastic pickguard.
▌ Six-saddle wrapover bridge/tailpiece.

STYLE EIGHTEEN (1979-81) USA

One pointed cutaway (and angled-in left upper bout) on small body

BEAST BST-1000 one-pickup 1979-81 *24-fret bolt-on neck, one pickup.*
▌ Bolt-on neck with unbound rosewood fingerboard, dot markers; 24 frets plus zero fret; truss-rod adjuster at headstock.
▌ Solid unbound body; brown (8210) or red (8216).
▌ One humbucker pickup.
▌ Two controls (volume, tone) and jack, all on pickguard.
▌ Colored plastic pickguard.

BODY STYLES
Each main model entry above includes a 'Style bar' to identify which of Gretsch's 20 distinctive body Styles is used. The styles are shown in silhouette, on the right, numbered 1 to 20.

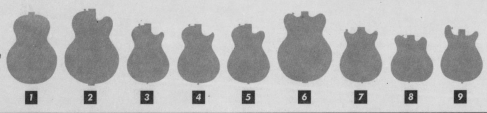

1 2 3 4 5 6 7 8 9

▌Six-saddle bridge/tailpiece with through-body stringing.
Also BEAST BST-1500 in brown (8217) from c1981.

BEAST BST-1000 two-pickup 1979-81 24-fret bolt-on neck.
Similar to BEAST BST-1000 one-pickup, except:
▌Red (8211) or brown (8215).
▌Two humbucker pickups.
▌Two controls (volume, tone), one selector and jack, all on pickguard.

BEAST BST-1500 See BEAST BST-1000 one-pickup listing.

STYLE NINETEEN (1979-80) USA

Twin pointed cutaways on small body

BEAST BST-2000 1979-80 22-fret bolt-on neck.
▌Bolt-on neck with unbound rosewood fingerboard, dot markers; 22 frets plus zero fret; truss-rod adjuster at headstock.
▌Solid unbound body; brown (8220) or red (8221).
▌Two humbuckers.
▌Two controls (volume, tone), one selector, one mini-switch and jack, all on pickguard.
▌Colored plastic pickguard.
▌Six-saddle bridge/tailpiece with through-body stringing.

STYLE TWENTY (1979-81) USA

Offset pointed cutaways on small body

BEAST BST-5000 1979-81 24-fret laminated through-neck on carved-edge body.
▌Laminated through-neck with bound rosewood fingerboard, dot markers; 24 frets plus zero fret; truss-rod adjuster at neck heel.

▌Solid carved-edge unbound body; brown (8250).
▌Two humbuckers.
▌Four controls (two volume, two tone), one selector and one mini switch.
▌Six-saddle bridge, separate bar tailpiece.

MISFITS, MAYBES, PROTOTYPES, POSSIBLES

As with other guitar makers, the Gretsch company was responsible for numerous one-offs, custom-built examples, evolving prototypes and special limited-production items (the latter often at the request of a dealer or individual customer). Many make frustratingly fleet appearances in Gretsch pricelists and literature with scant relevant information regarding specifications. The following is a list of the Gretsch guitars which seem to fit this 'could be' category. Some certainly existed in minimal numbers, and no doubt a few were made in at least small quantities, but others exist only in theory, usually as the result of some kind of misinformation.

BO DIDDLEY c1958-62
BO DIDDLEY CADILLAC c1961
BO DIDDLEY JUPITER c1961
BO DIDDLEY THUNDERBIRD c1961
CHET ATKINS JUNIOR c1969
CORVETTE (7623) c1976
CORVETTE II (7630) c1976-77
DELUXE CORVETTE (7632) c1976-77
HI ROLLER (7680) c1976
HI ROLLER (7685) c1978
ROC I (7635) c1976-77
ROY CLARK c1978
SAL FEBBRAIO c1967
SKINNY CHET (7680) c1974
7-11 SONGBIRD c1967
SOUTHERN BELLE (7176) c1983
STREAMLINER II (7667) c1973-75
SUPER ROC (7640) c1976-77
SUPER ROC II (7621) c1973-74

MISCELLANEOUS MAKES AND MODELS

Some guitars do not carry the Gretsch name prominently, but still have strong official connections with the company.

JAPAN

ELECTROMATIC by GRETSCH 1995-current
5120 Based on NASHVILLE 6120, see listing under STYLE TWO.
5122 Based on COUNTRY CLASSIC II 6122, see listing under STYLE SIX.
5128 Based on DUO JET 6128, see listing under STYLE THREE.
Cheaper equivalents made for Japanese domestic market only.

KOREA

TW (TRAVELING WILBURYS) 1989-90 One rounded cutaway small slab body with travel-theme graphics on front.
TW-100 One single-coil pickup, three-saddle bridge/tailpiece.
TW-100T Similar to TW-100, except: six-saddle bridge/vibrato unit.
TW-200 Similar to TW-100, except: two single-coil pickups.
TW-300 One humbucker pickup, six-saddle bridge/vibrato unit.
TW-500 Two single-coil pickups, six-saddle bridge/tailpiece.
TW-600 Similar to TW-500, except: six-saddle bridge/vibrato unit.
Inexpensive solidbody models issued as a marketing tie-in with The Traveling Wilburys 'supergroup' and featuring the Wilbury-alias autographs of members Bob Dylan, George Harrison, Jeff Lynne, Roy Orbison and Tom Petty.

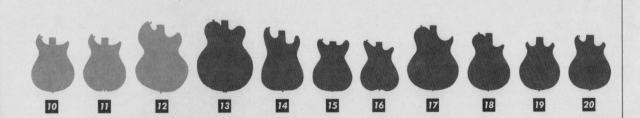

10 11 12 13 14 15 16 17 18 19 20

In addition to the Reference Listing, the following information may be of assistance.

MODEL NAMES

Some Gretsch models were at various times allotted a number of different names in company literature and pricelists. Those employed in the Reference Listing are deemed to be the official designations, as indicated by the nameplate or logo on the instruments themselves or by consistent use in Gretsch printed material. Some models may in fact be better known or equally well known by other names, and these have also been included and cross-referenced.

FRET COUNT

The number of frets can vary between examples of the same model. This has been noted in the Reference Listing where known, but additional variations may well exist.

PICKUPS

With Gretsch the company's use of single-coil or humbucker pickups at various times gives a clue to the instrument's period of production, and these two broad pickup types have therefore been identified within each entry in the Reference Listing. Various designs of single-coil and humbucker pickups have been employed by Gretsch over the years, but in the interests of clarity no such differences have been noted in the Reference Listing. In general on Gretsch guitars, a single-coil pickup can be identified by the presence of one row of six equally-spaced polepieces (see for example the Electro II with DeArmond pictured on pages 9-10 or the Corvette with HiLo'Tron on page 46). Humbuckers, on the other hand, employ dual coils, usually indicated by two rows of six equidistant polepieces (as on the White Falcon with Filter'Tron pages 33-35), or by twin laminated bar-poles (as on the Astro-Jet with Super'Tron page 55). The one exception to the latter is when a plated metal cover is fitted which allows only one row of six polepieces to be visible (as on TK300 with Japanese humbucker pages 70-71), a type featured on models in the 1970s.

COLORED PLASTIC PICKGUARD

In typical fashion, Gretsch often made effective use of colored plastic on its instruments, particularly for the pickguard, with gold and silver hues frequently replacing the more traditional black or tortoiseshell favored by other makers. However, inconsistencies abound, making it extremely difficult to allocate colors to certain models at specific times. So the definition 'Colored plastic pickguard' has been applied to all appropriate entries.

BRIDGES

Gretsch has employed a number of bridge designs over the years. In the interests of brevity these are not described in detail within the Reference Listing, but the various types include: Melita Synchrosonic (from about 1951; for example see the Electro II on page 9-10), 'Bigsby bar' (from about 1955; see the Hollow Body on the back of the jacket), Space Control (from about 1957; see White Falcon page 29), 'single metal bar' (from about 1957; see Hollow Body page 20-21), Floating Sound (from about 1965; see Viking page 62-63), Adjustamatic (from about 1970; see Country Club page 63), Terminator (from about 1975; see Committee page 71), as well as a handful of single-saddle wooden varieties.

SPECIAL ORDER OPTIONS

Many Gretsch guitars come with a separate vibrato tailpiece. Apart from a period during the early 1960s when a British-designed Burns unit was used on the solidbodies, Gretsch favored the US Bigsby-made types. This was sometimes listed as an option for certain models, although the Gretsch factory would fit a Bigsby to virtually any guitar if requested. The Bigsby vibrato tailpiece was equally easy to retro-fit and many Gretsches turn up with a Bigsby fitted by the owner subsequent to purchase. In view of all this, the presence of a separate vibrato tailpiece has only been noted when it was officially offered in Gretsch literature. Various different types of Bigsby units were used by Gretsch, but again in the interests of clarity these differences are not mentioned in the Reference Listing.

DATING GRETSCH GUITARS

Establishing the age of an instrument is an important necessity for most owners, especially those who possess vintage examples as often this aspect has a direct relationship to value. Many Gretsch models from the 1950s and 1960s have long been elevated to collectable status, thanks as much to their image and associations with famous players as to inherent quality.

Gretsch guitars, like those from virtually every other manufacturer, are hard to date with unquestioned exactitude, and an approximate age should be regarded as a safe and satisfying compromise.

Serial numbers can offer an indication of the production period, if not always a specific year. Using serial numbers as a sole method of dating is not advisable: numbering systems tend to be inconsistent or incomplete and can encompass confusing duplication or repetition. Such vagaries afflict the serial number schemes employed by most guitar makers, and Gretsch is certainly no exception. Other clues should wherever possible be used to confirm the age of a Gretsch guitar. Gretsch serial numbers can be on the headstock, or on a label inside the guitar.

GRETSCH SERIAL NUMBERS 1949-65 (USA)

Prior to 1949 Gretsch numbering was haphazard, with a series starting at 001 applied to only some of a predominantly acoustic line. In 1949 a new system was instituted for most models and this remained in use until 1965. Although on paper it appears straightforward, the numbers were not always applied in strict sequence or chronological order, and anachronistic anomalies can and do occur.

Number Series	Approx period
3000s	1949-50
4000s to 5000s	1951
5000s to 6000s	1952
6000s to 8000s	1953
9000s to 13,000s	1954
12,000s to 16,000s	1955
17,000s to 21,000s	1956
21,000s to 26,000s	1957
26,000s to 30,000s	1958
30,000s to 34,000s	1959
34,000s to 39,000s	1960
39,000s to 45,000s	1961
46,000s to 52,000s	1962
53,000s to 63,000s	1963
63,000s to 78,000s	1964
78,000s to 85,000s	1965

GRETSCH SERIAL NUMBERS 1965-72 (USA)

In 1965 the previous system was replaced by a new method which incorporated the date of manufacture. The number of digits used could vary from three to six: the first, or first and second, digit(s) indicate production month (from 1 to 12); the next digit denotes the last number of the relevant year (from 1965 to 1972); and any remaining digits are irrelevant.

For example:
592 suggests May (5) 1969 (9)
7820 suggests July (7) 1968 (8)
96220 suggests September (9) 1966 (6)
271376 suggests February (2) 1967 (7)

However, it should be noted that certain combinations can cause confusion regarding the date. Months 10, 11 and 12 (October, November and December respectively) could also indicate month 1 (January) and years 0, 1 and 2 (1970, 1971 and 1972 respectively). In such instances other dating pointers must be used to confirm true age.

102

GRETSCH SERIAL NUMBERS 1972-81 (USA)

The previous numbering scheme continued in operation until 1981, but from about 1972 the month digits were frequently separated from the rest of the serial number by a hyphen, or a dot, or a space.

This small difference helps to prevent any confusion regarding the year digit, which otherwise could often apply to both the 1965-72 and 1972-81 production periods. The visible presence of hyphen, dot or space within the number usually confirms that it relates to the latter time-span.

For example:
3-8094 suggests March (3) 1978 (8)
5.5125 suggests May (5) 1975 (5)
4 2126 suggests April (4) 1972 (2)

GRETSCH SERIAL NUMBERS 1989-current (Japan)

Since Gretsch guitar production recommenced in 1989 a different sequence has been used, comprising six digits plus a three-digit suffix. With typical Japanese logic, the first part provides the year of manufacture via the first two digits, while the fourth, fifth and sixth digits are part of the relevant model number.

For example:
901121-154 suggests 1990 (90), Round Up 6121 (*121*)
946119-982 suggests 1994 (*94*), Tennessee Rose 6119 (*119*)

OTHER DATING FEATURES

In addition to the serial number, a number of other features can be used to help in dating a Gretsch guitar – although the company, unlike some manufacturers, instituted comparatively few changes that affected the majority of the models in its line at any given time.

POSITION MARKERS

At first Gretsch electrics featured designs for fingerboard position markers that were already employed on their acoustic brethren: conventional dots or blocks, or the more distinctive and fancier 'hump-top' variation of blocks. While dots continued in use on cheaper Gretsches, the unique half-moon 'neo-classic' position markers were introduced to the remainder of the line in about 1957. These were used until 1981, but block markers were revived for some models around 1974. Gretsch used other types too, but only on certain instruments, so these do not serve as general dating pointers. At the time of writing, the current line features blocks, 'hump-top' blocks, and half-moon markers, used as appropriate to the original production period suggested by each of the new models.

ZERO FRET

This is a fret placed directly in front of the nut. It is used to determine string height, and thereby relegates the nut to a mere string guide. More commonly favored on instruments of European origin, the zero fret (fancifully described in company literature as the 'Action-flow fret nut') appeared on many Gretsch models from around 1959, remaining in use until 1981. It is employed on the current line, but only on the models pertinent to a certain original production period.

TRUSS-ROD ADJUSTER

On the majority of Gretsch models the truss-rod adjuster was originally located on the headstock, under a cover, but from about 1972 it was moved to a location behind the neck heel, accessed through the back of the body. This was the visible indication of a new truss-rod system, introduced by Gretsch's new owners, Baldwin, and previously used on guitars made by Burns, a British company acquired by Baldwin in 1965; Baldwin ceased production of Burns instruments in 1970. The Burns-designed 'gear-box'-controlled truss-rod then appeared on many Gretsch models until 1981.

MADE IN USA

Following the takeover of Gretsch by Baldwin in 1967, 'Made In USA' was stamped on the rear of the headstock, alongside the serial number. This continued until about 1973.

BODY

Gretsch followed Gibson's fashion by introducing twin-cutaway styling on various of its popular hollow body and semi-solidbody models from about 1961. The semi-solids reverted to single-cutaway design around eight years later, again reflecting the popularity of Gibson designs. Gretsch employed very large f-holes on many of its hollow body guitars until the early 1960s when the size was slightly reduced, and from c1972 they became smaller again. 'Fake' f-holes (blocked-in or painted-on f-holes) were a unique Gretsch feature introduced on certain models around 1957, but these were replaced by the real thing from about 1972.

PICKUPS

Around 1957 Gretsch introduced a humbucking pickup to replace the single-coil type made for them by DeArmond. Hitherto this had been the choice for all Gretsch's electrics. The new Filter'Tron pickup was featured on many models from then on, later being joined by other humbucker units such as the Super'Tron around 1963. Conversely, in about 1960 Gretsch came up with its own single-coil pickup, the Hi-Lo'Tron, and this was then employed on various cheaper hollow body and solidbody instruments. The current line features revised versions of the Filter'Tron humbucker and DeArmond-style single-coil pickups as appropriate to 'vintage'.

CONTROLS AND CIRCUITRY

Partnering the launch of the new Filter'Tron humbucker pickup came a revised circuitry system. Gretsch abandoned its previous conventional rotary tone controls and instead fitted toggle-type selectors providing preset tonal changes. From around 1970 the company returned to normal tone controls, but for some models only; others retained the tone selectors until 1981. The current line employs both types of control layout, again relevant to the original production period being revived by each model. Another date-relevant control component was the standby switch, a unique Gretsch feature. This addition to many upscale models, used from about 1961 to 1978, allowed the instrument to be turned off without disconnecting the cord. Again this is employed on the current models where appropriate.

PICKGUARD

From about 1972 a more angular, 'squared-off' style of pickguard replaced the original curvaceous Gretsch design, and this is one of the very few changes made that is common to virtually all models.

CONTROL POT CODES

The metal casings of many American-made control potentiometers (usually called 'pots') are stamped with code numbers which include date information, and these can therefore provide useful confirmation of an instrument's age. However, be aware that pots were not always used immediately, and also that they may have been replaced at some time – factors which could cause contradiction and confusion. The code comprises six or seven numbers. Of these the first three identify the manufacturer and can be disregarded, while the final two indicate the week of the production year and are equally unimportant for our purposes. In a six-digit code it is the fourth number which indicates the last digit of the appropriate year during the 1950s period: 195?. In a seven-digit code, the fourth and fifth numbers signify the last two digits of any year thereafter.

MODELS & YEARS

This listing shows the models produced by Gretsch, in chronological order of production. The number in the box refers to the body shape style.

USA

	Model	Years
1	Electromatic Spanish 1st	1939-42
1	Electromatic Spanish 2nd	1949-54
1	Electro II 1st	1951-54
2	Electro II 2nd	1951-54
2	Electromatic	1951-54
3	Duo Jet 1st	1953-61
2	Chet Atkins Hollow Body 1st	1955-61
3	Chet Atkins Solid Body 1st	1955-61
1	Corvette hollow body version	1954-56
2	Country Club 1st, 2nd, 3rd & 4th	1954-81
3	Round Up	1954-59
3	Silver Jet 1st	1954-61
2	Streamliner 1st	1954-59
2	Convertible	1955-59
3	Jet Fire Bird 1st	1955-61
2	White Falcon 1st	1955-62
3	White Penguin 1st	1955-61
1	Clipper 1st	1956-58
2	Chet Atkins Country Gentleman 1st	1957-61
2	Clipper 2nd & 3rd	1957-74
4	Rambler 1st	1957-60
2	Anniversary one-pickup	1958-72
2	Anniversary two-pickup 1st, 2nd & 3rd	1958-77
2	Chet Atkins Tennessean 1st, 2nd & 3rd	1958-79
2	Country Club Stereo 1st & 2nd	1958-65
2	White Falcon Stereo 1st & 2nd	1958-62

	Model	Years
2	Sal Salvador	1959-66
5	Rambler 2nd version	1960-62
2	Anniversary Stereo	1961-63
8	Bikini	1961
6	Chet Atkins Country Gentleman 2nd & 3rd	1961-81
6	Chet Atkins Hollow Body 2nd	1961-67
7	Chet Atkins Solid Body 2nd	1961-62
9	Corvette solidbody 1st	1961-62
7	Duo Jet 2nd	1961-69
7	Jet Fire Bird 2nd	1961-69
7	Silver Jet 2nd	1961-63
7	White Penguin 2nd	1961-62
10	Corvette solidbody 2nd, one-pickup	1962-65
10	Princess	1962-63
6	Ronny Lee	1962-63
10	Twist	1962-63
6	White Falcon 2nd & 3rd	1962-80
6	White Falcon Stereo 3rd & 4th	1962-81
12	Astro-Jet	1963-66
10	Corvette solidbody 2nd, two-pickup	1963-65
2	'Cat's-Eye Custom'	1964-67
6	Viking 1st & 2nd	1964-75
11	Corvette solidbody 3rd, one-pickup	1965-68
11	Corvette solidbody 3rd, two-pickup	1965-70
6	Monkees	1966-67
6	12-string	1966-70
6	Black Hawk	1967-70
6	Chet Atkins Nashville 1st & 2nd	1967-79
6	Rally	1967-68
6	Sam Goody	1967

	Model	Years
6	Streamliner 2nd & 3rd	1967-75
2	Van Eps seven-string 1st & 2nd	1968-78
2	Van Eps six-string	1968-72
3	Roc Jet 1st & 2nd	1969-79
13	Deluxe Chet	1972-73
13	Super Chet	1972-79
3	Roc II	1973-75
3	Country Roc	1974-79
2	White Falcon 4th	1974-78
2	White Falcon Stereo 5th	1974-78
6	Broadkaster semi-hollow body 1st & 2nd	1975-79
14	Broadkaster solidbody	1975-76
17	Atkins Axe	1977-80
15	Committee	1977-81
17	Super Axe	1977-80
16	TK 300	1977-81
18	Beast BST-1000	1979-81
19	Beast BST-2000	1979-80
20	Beast BST-5000	1979-81
18	Beast BST-1500	1981
6	Country Squire	1981
2	Country Club 1955 Custom	1995-current
2	Nashville 1955 Custom	1995-current
2	White Falcon I – 1955 Custom	1995-current

JAPAN

	Model	Years
2	Country Classic I	1989-current
6	Country Classic II 6122	1989-current
3	Duo Jet 6128	1989-current
3	Jet Firebird	1989-current

	Model	Years
2	Nashville 6120	1989-current
2	Nashville Western 6120W	1989-current
3	Round Up	1989-current
3	Silver Jet 6129	1989-current
2	Tennessee Rose 6119	1989-current
2	White Falcon 6136	1990-current
2	White Falcon 7593	1990-current
6	White Falcon 7594	1990-current
2	Black Falcon 6136BK	1992-current
2	Black Falcon 7593BK	1992-current
6	Black Falcon 7594BK	1992-current
2	Nashville 6120-1960	1992-current
2	Rancher 6022CV	1992-current
2	Synchromatic 400MCV	1992-current
2	Anniversary one-pickup	1993-current
2	Anniversary two-pickup	1993-current
6	Country Classic II 6122-1962	1993-current
2	Nashville Brian Setzer	1993-current
2	Tennessee Rose 6119-1962	1993-current
3	White Penguin	1993-94
3	Duo Jet 6128-1957	1994-current
3	Silver Jet 6129-1957	1994-current
2	Synchromatic 6040MC-SS	1994-current
17	Axe	1995-current
2	Silver Falcon 6136SL	1995-current
6	Silver Falcon 7594SL	1995-current
3	Sparkle Jet 6129	1995-current
3	Sparkle Jet 6129-1957	1995-current

OWNERS' CREDITS

Guitars photographed came from the following individuals' collections, and we are most grateful for their help.

The owners are listed here in the alphabetical order of the code used to identify their guitars in the Key To Guitar Photographs below.

AH Adrian Hornbrook; **AR** Alan Rogan; **AV** Arthur Vitale; **CA** Chet Atkins; **CC** The Chinery Collection; **CL** Charlie Lasham; **DC** Don Clayton; **DE** Duane Eddy; **DG** David Gilmour; **FG** Fred Gretsch Enterprises; **GG** Gruhn Guitars; **GH** George Harrison; **JB** Jeff Beck; **JC** Jennifer Cohen; **JR** John Reynolds; **JS** John Sheridan; **LW** Lew Weston; **MB** Mandolin Bros; **MG** Music Ground; **MW** Michael Wright; **PD** Paul Day; **PI** Peter Ilowite; **RB** Ray Butts; **SA** Scot Arch; **SH** Steve Howe; **SR** Sunrise Guitars.

KEY TO GUITAR PHOTOGRAPHS

The following key is designed to identify who owned which guitars when they were photographed for this book. After the relevant page number (*in italic type*) we list: the model and where necessary other identifier, followed by the owner's initials in **bold type** (see Owners' Credits above). For example, '2/3 White Falcon 1958 **SA**' means that the 1958 White Falcon shown across pages 2 and 3 was owned by Scot Arch.

Jacket front: White Falcon 1955 **SA**, Round Up 1994 **FG**. *Inside front jacket flap:* 'Silver Jet' 1969 **SA**. 2/3: White Falcon 1958 **SA**; Jet Fire Bird 1958 **DG**. 6: Hollow Body **JR**; headstocks Electro II 1954 **LW**, White Falcon 1955 **SA**. 9/10: Electro II **LW**, Corvette **MB**. 10: Country Clubs both **CC**. 11/12/13: Hollow Body proto **CA**. 12/13: Hollow Body **CA**. 13: Hollow Body **SA**; Solid Body **LW**. 16/17: Duo Jet **GG**; Silver Jet **SA**. 17: Jet Fire Bird **AR**; Duo Jet **JB**. 20/21: Hollow Body **DE**. 21: Hollow Body **GG**. 24: Streamliner tan **AV**; Streamliner yellow/brown **JR**; Convertible **CC**. 25: Clipper **JR**; White Falcon **AH**. 28/29: White Penguin 1956 **CC**; White Penguin 1958 **DG**. 29: White Falcon **GG**. 31: White Falcon Stereo **SA**. 31/32: Country Club Stereo **JR**. 32: Hollow Body custom **CC**; Silver Jet testbed **RB**. 33/34/35: White Falcon Stereo 1966 **JC**. 35: White Falcon Stereo 1962 **JR**. 38/39: Anniversary **AH**; Anniversary detail **GG**. 39: Tennessean **GG**; Country Gent **GG**. 42/43: Hollow Body red **CC**; Ronny Lee **CL**. 43: Hollow Body twin-cut **JR**. 46: Corvette **DC**; Twist **SR**. 47: 'Silver Jet' **SA**; 'Gold Jet' **DG**. 50/51: Duo Jet **GG**; Country Gent **SA**. 51: Country Gent **LW**; Nashville **LW**. 54: 'Gold Duke' **PI**; 'Silver Duke' **PI**. 55: Roc Jet **LW**; Bikini **SH**; Astro-Jet **PD**. 58/59: 12-string **JS**; Monkees **JS**. 59: Rally **GG**. 62/63: Van Eps **MG**; Viking **MG**. 63: White Falcon 1975 **MB**; White Falcon 1980 **GG**; Country Club **GG**. 66/67: Super Chet **CA**; Hi Roller **JS**. 67: Country Gent custom **CA**; Atkins Axe **CA**. 70/71: TK 300 **PD**; Beast **MW**. 71: Committee **MW**; Country Roc **PD**. 74: Traveling Wilburys **PD**; Nashville Setzers both **FG**. 75: All **FG**. *Jacket back:* Hollow Body 1955 **AH**.

Guitar photography was by Miki Slingsby, with the exception of: Astro-Jet p55, TK 300 p70/1, Country Roc p71 and Traveling Wilburys p74 (Garth Blore); two Nashville Setzers, Silver Jet, Country Classic II, Duo Jet and Blue Pearl Sparkle Jet (Loft Marketing).

MEMORABILIA illustrated in this book, including catalogs, brochures, magazines, record sleeves, sketches, blueprints and photographs (in fact anything that isn't a guitar) came from the collections of Scot Arch, Chet Atkins, Tony Bacon, Ray Butts, The Chinery Collection, Jennifer Cohen, Paul Day, Duane Eddy, Ross Finley, Gruhn Guitars, Adrian Hornbrook, The Music Trades, The National Jazz Archive (Loughton) and Alan Rogan. These finely textured items were transformed for your enjoyment by Miki Slingsby.

INTERVIEWS

We are very grateful to the many individuals who consented to be interviewed for this book. The great majority of quotations in the text are from original interviews conducted by Tony Bacon, and most were arranged especially for *The Gretsch Book*.

Subjects were: Chet Atkins (April 1995, May 1995); Ray Butts (April 1995); Jennifer Cohen (April 1995); Dan Duffy (September 1995); Duane Eddy (April 1995); Ross Finley (April 1995); Phil Grant (August 1995); Fred Gretsch III (June 1995); Bill Hagner (July 1995); Dick Harrison (July 1995, September 1995); Dale Hyatt (February 1992); Duke Kramer (March 1995); Ted McCarty (October 1992); Don Randall (February 1992); Dean Turner (March 1995).

The quotation from 'When I Play On My Gretsch Guitar' is copyright Rialto Music. The quotations by Steve Stills and George Harrison are from *Guitar Player*. The sources of the few other previously published quotations are given where they occur in the text.

IN ADDITION to those named above in OWNERS' CREDITS and in INTERVIEWS we would like to thank: Les Barrett; Julie Bowie; Bill Bush; Ann Butts; Mike Carey; Walter Carter; Clarissa Cater; Scott Chinery; Bruce Cohen; Jane, Sarah & Simon Day; Deed Eddy; Ethel Ettinger; Justin Harrison (Music Ground); Rick Harrison (Music Ground); Vincent Hastwell; Jim Hilmar; Stan Jay (Mandolin Bros); Paul Johnson (Gruhn Guitars); Ken Jones (National Jazz Archive); Ronny Lee; Brian Majeski (The Music Trades); Phil Moon (Loft Marketing); The Nashville Mandolin Ensemble; Outlaw Guitars; Ted Rothstein; Andrea T Sheridan; Steve Soest (Soest Guitar Repair); Arthur Soothill (Tuned Percussion); Sally Stockwell; George Van Eps; Larry Wexer (Mandolin Bros); Paul Yandel.

BIBLIOGRAPHY

Tony Bacon & Paul Day *The Fender Book* (IMP/Miller Freeman 1992), *The Gibson Les Paul Book* (IMP/Miller Freeman 1993), *The Rickenbacker Book* (IMP/Miller Freeman 1994), *The Ultimate Guitar Book* (DK/Knopf 1991); Tony Bacon & Barry Moorhouse *The Bass Book* (IMP/Miller Freeman 1995); Robert & Celia Dearling *The Guinness Book Of Recorded Sound* (Guinness 1984); A R Duchossoir *Gibson Electrics - The Classic Years* (Hal Leonard 1994), *Guitar Identification* (Hal Leonard 1990); Hugh Gregory *1000 Great Guitarists* (IMP/Miller Freeman 1994); George Gruhn & Walter Carter *Gruhn's Guide To Vintage Guitars* (GPI 1991), *Electric Guitars And Basses* (GPI 1994); Steve Howe & Tony Bacon *The Steve Howe Guitar Collection* (IMP/Miller Freeman 1994); Colin Larkin (editor) *The Guinness Encyclopedia Of Popular Music* (Guinness 1992); Mark Lewisohn *The Complete Beatles Recording Sessions* (Hamlyn 1988), *The Complete Beatles Chronicle* (Pyramid 1992); Dave McAleer (editor) *The Book Of Hit Singles* (Carlton 1994); Norman Mongan *The History Of The Guitar In Jazz* (Oak 1983); John Morrish *The Fender Amp Book* (IMP/Miller Freeman 1995); Jay Scott *Gretsch: The Guitars Of The Fred Gretsch Company* (Centerstream 1992); Paul Trynka (editor) *The Electric Guitar* (Virgin 1993); Tom Wheeler *American Guitars* (HarperPerennial 1990); YMM Player *History Of Electric Guitars* (Player Corporation 1988).

We also consulted back issues of the following magazines: *Beat Instrumental* (UK); *Beat Monthly* (UK); *Country & Western Jamboree* (US); *Down Beat* (US); *Guitar Magazine* (UK); *Guitar Player* (US); *Guitarist* (UK); *Making Music* (UK); *The Music Trades* (US); *One Two Testing* (UK); *Vintage Gallery* (US); *Vintage Guitar Magazine* (US); *20th Century Guitar* (US).

Jacket pictures
Front: 1955 White Falcon (body); 1994 Round Up (neck); Jimmie Webster portrait, out-take from 1955 catalog session; That Great Gretsch sound 1968 catalog cover; strumming White Falcon on 1972 catalog cover.
Back: 1955 Chet Atkins Hollow Body and case; Gretsch letter heading 1957; OK Card 1963; Brian Setzer ad 1994; various color finish swatches.
Inside flap: 'Silver Jet' 1969.

Contents page pictures White Falcon 1958; 1955 catalog cover; Jet Fire Bird 1958; Mary Osborne 1957; Arrow-through-G knob blueprint 1957; Gretsch Thin plectrum; padded back; arrow-through-G knob.

The Gretsch Book has passed all quality control tests and is ready for shipment.